Media, Internet, and Social Movements in Hong Kong

I0421932

Focusing on the unique story of the "recolonisation" of Hong Kong since 2019, this book describes the environment of news gathering and publishing during this period and studies how this has connected to wider political, economic, and social changes.

Media, Internet, and Social Movements in Hong Kong considers the operation of the news media in this divided region to illuminate the unparalleled experience of the transfer of sovereignty of the territory from a liberal democracy to a semi-authoritarian regime. This book examines key aspects of news production that constrain media freedom in the Hong Kong Special Administrative Region (HKSAR) including the routines and concrete cases of censorship exercised by state authorities, self-censorship by news organisations, and the roles of the Chinese and HKSAR governments as key sources of news. The authors also discuss the norms and values of journalists and citizens in Hong Kong as forces resisting control as well as the popular use of social media in mobilising anti-government protests.

This compelling text will be of interest to students and scholars in the fields of journalism, media, and area studies, particularly those focusing on Greater China and the Asia-Pacific region.

Carol P. Lai is a retired Associate Professor in Global Communication Program at Akita International University, Japan.

Andrew Y. To is a retired Assistant Professor in the Department of Journalism at Hong Kong Baptist University.

Routledge Focus on Communication and Society
Series Editor: James Curran

Routledge Focus on Communication and Society offers both established and early-career academics the flexibility to publish cutting-edge analysis on topical issues, research on new media or in-depth case studies within the broad field of media, communication and cultural studies. Its main concerns are whether the media empower or fail to empower popular forces in society; media organisations and public policy; and the political and social consequences of the media.

For more information about this series, please visit: https://www.routledge.com/Routledge-Focus-on-Communication-and-Society/book-series/00RFCS

Media, Internet, and Social Movements in Hong Kong

Control and Protest

Carol P. Lai and Andrew Y. To

Routledge
Taylor & Francis Group

LONDON AND NEW YORK

First published 2025
by Routledge
4 Park Square, Milton Park, Abingdon, Oxon OX14 4RN

and by Routledge
605 Third Avenue, New York, NY 10158

Routledge is an imprint of the Taylor & Francis Group, an informa business

© 2025 Carol P. Lai and Andrew Y. To

The right of Carol P. Lai and Andrew Y. To to be identified as authors of this work has been asserted in accordance with sections 77 and 78 of the Copyright, Designs and Patents Act 1988.

British Library Cataloguing-in-Publication Data
A catalogue record for this book is available from the British Library

Library of Congress Cataloging-in-Publication Data
Names: Lai, Carol P. (Carol Pui-Yee), 1958- author. | To, Andrew Y, author.
Title: Media, internet, and social movements in Hong Kong : control and protest / Carol P. Lai and Andrew Y. To.
Description: 1st. | London ; New York : Routledge, 2025. | Series: Routledge focus on communication and society | Includes bibliographical references and index.
Identifiers: LCCN 2024016904 (print) | LCCN 2024016905 (ebook) | ISBN 9780367713027 (hardback) | ISBN 9780367713010 (paperback) | ISBN 9781003150244 (ebook)
Subjects: LCSH: Journalism--Social aspects--China--Hong Kong. | Press--China--Hong Kong--History--21st century. | Mass media--China--Hong Kong. | Government and the press--China--Hong Kong--History--21st century.
Classification: LCC PN4748.C5 L355 2025 (print) | LCC PN4748.C5 (ebook) | DDC 302.23095125--dc23/eng/20240617
LC record available at https://lccn.loc.gov/2024016904
LC ebook record available at https://lccn.loc.gov/2024016905

ISBN: 9780367713027 (hbk)
ISBN: 9780367713010 (pbk)
ISBN: 9781003150244 (ebk)

DOI: 10.4324/9781003150244

Typeset in Times New Roman
by Deanta Global Publishing Services, Chennai, India

Contents

Foreword

Tim Hamlett

This is a book about the role of the media in recent events in Hong Kong, and how various theories about media use and influence can be applied to this history. Carol P. Lai is well qualified to write such a book, having had a successful career in both journalism and media education. Qualifications and experience are however not enough; in the present circumstances of Hong Kong such an enterprise also requires courage. Like many Hongkongers Ms Lai finds that her memories of recent events do not always overlap with the version of history currently propagated by the Hong Kong government and its supporters. One of the noticeable changes of the last few years is that the government has become much more resistant and resentful of criticism, or even of disagreement. It has also been resourceful and ingenious in finding new ways of making its displeasure felt.

As an occasional commentator on Hong Kong affairs I have been distressed to find how often lately I am exploring territory already mapped long ago by George Orwell. This book is not just a contribution to learnt discourse on media matters. It is also an attempt to prevent, or at least delay, Hong Kong's arrival at the destination outlined in *1984*, where

> Every record has been destroyed or falsified, every book rewritten, every picture has been repainted, every statue and street building has been renamed, every date has been altered. And the process is continuing day by day and minute by minute. History has stopped. Nothing exists except an endless present in which the Party is always right.

1 Introduction

In an earlier study of Hong Kong media and regime change, the significance of media professionalism and media organisation, the role of the media in political change, and the relationship between the media and a society's power base were explored, taking Hong Kong as an example.[1] This previous work adopted a historical, political, and economic approach in its exploration of the Hong Kong press in three significant periods: under colonial rule in the late 1960s; during the political transition to Chinese rule in the 1990s; and in the post-handover period in the early 2000s. As mentioned in that study, radical political economists tend to view capitalist society as being class dominated.[2] The media is seen as part of an ideological arena in which various class ideas are contested. Although dominated by certain classes, ultimate control is increasingly exercised by the monopoly of capital. Analysts of this tradition are concerned that the increasing concentration of power coincides with dominant political and economic interests. The media operate within the framework of the dominant power structure and are dependent upon the dominant ideology, which in turn reflects and reinforces the status quo.

In contrast, according to the liberal tradition, the media respond to, and reflect, the views and values of the public, thus ensuring consumer control. The liberal theorists' view differs significantly from that of the radicals. While the radical approach emphasises media censorship and self-censorship, the liberal approach emphasises the control that consumers can exercise through market forces. The central liberal idea is that the general shape and nature of the press is ultimately determined by readers, through the hidden hand of the free market. Thus liberal theorists tend to see the media as neutral, independent, and owing allegiance to the public interest rather than to the organised political interests of society. However, historical analysis reveals more complex situations than these two positions propose. The findings of the last study had a number of theoretical implications. First, one strand of the Western political/economic argument emphasises market censorship. It sees control as being exercised primarily through economic processes. What that study revealed, however, was that political power was a key influence in shaping the Hong Kong press.

***

DOI: 10.4324/9781003150244-1

Drawing on the lessons drawn from the Hong Kong experience in the last study, we can reconstruct the paradigm of radical political economy in order to make allowances for elements of the liberal democracy models (such as the role of professional norms and standards, public expectations and aspirations, and the power of civil society) which counteract the infrastructural/economic factors and superstructural/political reasons that impinge on press freedom. The experience of Hong Kong, where the first HKSAR Chief Executive in 2003 had not been able to carry out his mandate fully and where elite opinion was split over major government policies (such as on the enactment of the proposed new national security law), suggests that the power of agents and actors (such as the pan-democratic alliance) may override the dominant power of economic control and political censorship. The overwhelming importance of political and economic reality in shaping media content can subsequently be undermined.

However, we can also rework the liberal democracy model to take seriously into account the overwhelming importance of political and economic reality in shaping media content. In my reconstructed account of the liberal democratic model during the colonial suppression in the 1960s, although the media system was a relatively open and competitive process in which various actors were competing for influence, the political power of the British colonial administration and economic ownership combined to produce media content that was biased or class-biased against the underdog/underprivileged, and in favour of the ruling political and economic elites. In short, in that study I attempted to argue that the larger environment of Hong Kong was changing rapidly. So too was public sentiment. However, the political culture, journalistic norms, and institutional support remained strong. It is evident that the British colonial government was highly oppressive at one point, but it also changed enormously over time.

Although the Chinese regime is an authoritarian regime in nature, it has been adjusting its strategy, if not entirely its policy, towards Hong Kong. As has already been pointed out, media organisations are subjected to influences that can make them conform to the establishment's ideology. The media in liberal democracies are often subjected to influence from above and below. How these pressures and constraints are manifested, and whether countervailing forces are present in a vigorous form, however, depends upon the specific circumstances. In a bureaucratic, capitalistic 'autonomous region' such as Hong Kong, which is a transitional society and largely deviates from the static model of a Western liberal democracy, as well as being a subordinate territory to a government with no commitment to press freedom, the interaction is even more complex.

***

Two decades later, in the wake of the vigorous general uprising in 2019, it is proposed to write a manuscript on the topic of 'media, internet, and social movements in Hong Kong: control and protest' with the aim of re-examining the role of media in this unprecedented movement. In particular, we should look at the spread of information, mobilisation of ordinary people's participation, escalation of dissenting opinion, and changing perceptions. More importantly, we can consider whether the media can perform as a countervailing force with other civil society stakeholders. In hindsight, the movement in 2019 appears as very much a continuation of the movement in 2003, when the last study was conducted. Again, the unrest was triggered by the promulgation of a National Security Law with a new name: "extradition amendment bill." In the wake of the unprecedented social movement in 2019, the Hong Kong extradition amendment bill was indefinitely shelved, but then one year after on 1 July 2020, a mainland National Security Bill, which was much worse, was imposed.

To a large extent, the protest in 2019 was very much devoted to pursuing democracy in a broad sense – to strive for a free press, freedom of assembly, and ultimately to pursue universal suffrage: for the people's representatives in the Legislative Council as well as the Chief Executive of HKSAR to be elected by the people at large. However, the movement in 2019 also featured a change in strategy from the protest side. There was a focus on the newly found political awareness and swift consolidation of local identity. There was cohesion to avoid splits between political stakeholders insisting on peaceful means and those adopting fast-changing and radical means, with both camps at the same time riding on the democratic media advocacy wagon. We shall thus make the distinction and attempt to analyse the grey areas and different levels of media immersion as they arise in the following chapters, which, we should say, is the most intriguing part of this attempt at analysis. Plenty of research has already been conducted on the subject of social movements, and also the role and function of the media in fuelling general sentiments in the course of the happenings in many places over the last few years. It is still a bold attempt to document and research on this Hong Kong movement from the angle of media and power, in particular as the effects of the government's response are only beginning to be felt strongly at the fifth anniversary of the movement.

In the wake of the authorities' attempt to wipe out history and memory, and to re-narrate evidence of civic conflicts and colonial civil remnants, it is especially important to record and analyse freshly surfaced and revealing information. Hundreds of media practitioners and thousands of movement protesters or dissidents have been jailed for years, or have already fled to foreign countries seeking political asylum or residence. Those who have remained in Hong Kong for various personal and political reasons are under tremendous pressure at this hostile juncture. The newly promulgated Chinese-style National Security Law put into effect in 2020 turned out in practice to have a retrospective effect, although the authorities previously said it would not.

On top of the mainland-imposed national security law, another lethal blow to the media in Hong Kong is the newly passed local National Security Law – the enactment of Article 23 of Hong Kong mini-constitution, the Basic Law, in 2024. With these escalating legal measures to rein in critical opinion and in particular to silence oppositional or alternative views, society has become relatively quiet in comments and opinions circulated in traditional media as well as on social media platforms. There was a high-profile consultation exercise on the enactment of Article 23 of the Basic Law conducted, with the arrival of a top Beijing official and his entourage to check on local sentiment.[3] However, even minor comments or criticisms were loudly denounced as not conducive to a successful exercise, and not supportive of the administration's national security efforts.[4] The Hong Kong Journalists Association's submission was a rare local expression of concern about the potential impact of Article 23 on journalists. While overseas activist groups, led by UK-based organisation Hong Kong Watch, issued a joint statement condemning the proposed security law, opposition in the city has been muted.[5]

In view of this latest development, this manuscript remains not so much about the movement itself and its political and social aspects, as about the media's part in the course of events. Among news media in general, we shall focus particularly on *Apple Daily* and *Stand News*, given their prominent role and influence as they were the leading democratic media, in terms of their huge circulation and popularity. But we shall also touch on other media if they are relevant to the discussion. *Apple Daily* and *Stand News* were regarded as carrying significant weight by the establishment side because of their supposed impact on the movement, the general audience and the authorities. There is also further evidence of their significance as the authorities would label the proprietor of *Apple Daily* as the "ringleader" or "mastermind", and *Stand News* as "plan B of the *Apple Daily*" when they were targeted, raided, and forced to shut down with their assets and bank deposits frozen, while the top management, including senior journalists, were detained for more than two years and faced up to life imprisonment if convicted.

This book will not be able to analyse the outcome of the trial now being conducted while writing is in progress. But we can explore and analyse the enormous effect and energy in the information the two media outlets offered during the entire movement, which lasted for more than half a year. And it is not too soon during the trial of the people in question – attracting not only domestic but also global attention in 2023 and 2024 – for an attempt to analyse, in Chapters 3 and 4 respectively, the control mechanisms imposed by the authorities and the protester strategies which provoked them. In short, this is not a comprehensive manuscript on the movement itself, which time and resources do not permit. More importantly, such a history is discouraged by the political hostility exerted as social control since the all-powerful National Security Law was promulgated. Thus in the author's interviews with relevant sources, the identity of the interviewee will be protected, and the time and place where the interview took place will be withheld in order to protect the interviewees as well as the author himself or herself. In this connection, we shall be sticking to material already published as far as possible.

The outline of this manuscript has been revised to fit in what we think best reflects the issues and the topics we touch upon. The political economy media theory which was elaborated in the previous book, *Media in Hong Kong: Press Freedom and Regime Change*, led to the conclusion that Hong Kong could retain its relative freedom of speech and press freedom, but whether this happened would by and large hinge on mainland China's development and its adherence to the pledge of "one country two systems." Chapter 2 will focus on "one country, two systems," its effect and deterioration and its subsequent impact on the well-being of Hong Kong as a global city and an information hub. Chapter 3, "Media, Internet and the Civil Movement: Part 1 Control," will mainly focus on the legal and extra-legal means to which the authorities resorted, and analyse how this strategy fuelled further resentment and pushed the movement to a level which was out of control and unimaginable in the past. The authorities also started to use more subtle means: deniable operations by "spontaneous" supporters, and tactics such as interrogation, stalking, and use of intermediaries to harass or befriend – the so-called carrot and stick strategy. In Chapter 4, "Media, Internet and the Civil Movement: Part 2 Protest," we shall attempt to analyse the characteristics and essence of the social movement in 2019, which was largely a continuation of previous movements in 2003, 2012, and 2014, but was also innovative. The objectives of the movement treated localism as a natural complement to democracy. It deployed a new strategy of decentralised leadership and specifically rejected the traditional approaches of the Hong Kong pan-democrats: the "compromise and criticise" attitude to the authorities and seeing reunification with greater China as a viable road to democracy.

The new generation of protesters, which had briefly sprouted and tasted an early success in the protests against the National and Moral Education scheme in 2012, learnt their lesson in the bitter-sweet romantic Umbrella Movement or Occupy Central Movement in 2014. Then came the explosive 2019 anti-extradition movement which caught them by surprise, but they swiftly revised their tactics to deploy spontaneity and flexibility, while dispensing with traditional ideas like having a big platform agreed by all, or depending on a prominent leader. Instead they used social media and devices such as Telegram and Lihkg to connect with up to 200,000 friends or strangers at a time, to swiftly build up action plans and make it difficult for the authorities to clamp down. This was the so-called "be water" movement. There were also all kinds of innovative and cultural forms, such as Lennon Walls on which people could express individual opinions by putting up memo stickers, by singing a song adopted from the *Les Miserables* musical – "Do you hear the people sing," by inventing "lunch with you," "chain with you," and later creating their own Hong Kong alternative anthem "Glory to Hong Kong" which generated soft power to support their pursuit of Hong Kong democracy. Their willingness to sacrifice their time, studies, careers, futures, and even their lives indeed impressed many ordinary citizens who had initially no intention of joining a movement of any kind. Many eventually took to the streets for the first time to air their grievances, anger, and aspiration for the long-standing hope of democracy. We shall analyse this situation, to see whether market theory can be applied or not.

Chapter 5 is a retrospective summary of the points made so far and a look at the future. With the above setting and evidence, we shall come up with a preliminary prospect of the relationship among media, the internet, and social movement in the case of Hong Kong.

Notes

1 Carol P. Lai, *Media in Hong Kong: Press Freedom and Political Change 1967–2005*, London: Routledge, 2007.
2 Ibid., chapter 1.
3 Felix Tam, China Says Hong Kong's "One Country, Two Systems" Is Permanent, SCMP Reports, *Yahoo*, 27 February 2024, accessed at: https://news.yahoo.com/china-says-hong-kong-one-235724549.html?guccounter=1&guce_referrer=a HR0cHM6Ly93d3cuZ29vZ2xlLmNvbvbS8&guce_referrer_sig=AQAAAKnVBf-y CjNoILTqbU1Mz3gZPzq7tGkJhYcgG4ZLqihZaDGt2yKjEbD42UkZDZIR0sTx CiCAQOR1TLTURo_TTV2nOxy_A0YmAqTueeJ1djC5zspxrNXvcEFy83Q OsMzuNs0rSiLILX_my3Azgj54fblVZzXZEjZHBIO-3C9mJadP
4 Hillary Leung, Article 23: New Domestic Security Law May Affect Regular News Reporting, Says Hong Kong Press Group, *Hong Kong Free Press*, 26 February 2024, accessed at: https://hongkongfp.com/2024/02/26/article-23-new-domestic-security-law-may-affect-regular-news-reporting-says-hong-kong-press-group/
5 Ibid.

2 Autonomy seized, democracy denied, and destiny failed

How the Chinese Communist Party's Hong Kong policy caused the early death of "one country, two systems"

Andrew Y. To

Introduction: A promise and its betrayal

Hong Kong was once the promised land for the pursuit of democratic self-rule under China's sovereignty. By the formula of "one country, two systems" (OCTS), stipulated in the Sino-British Joint Declaration (the Declaration), an international agreement,[1] Hong Kong would become China's Special Administrative Region (SAR) in 1997 but enjoy a high degree of autonomy. Hong Kong people would run Hong Kong, largely free from Beijing intervention, while its social and economic systems would remain unchanged for 50 years. With fundamental rights and freedoms ensured by law, and property rights protected, Hong Kong would remain a free capitalistic cosmopolitan city open to the world. Besides the pre-1997 status quo for at least 50 years were undertakings that included: the Court of Final Appeal would have the power of final judgment on legal disputes, the Chief Executive would be returned by elections or consultations held in Hong Kong, and the legislature would be constituted by elections. In drafting the Basic Law of Hong Kong Special Administrative Region (henceforth Basic Law), the SAR mini-constitution, Beijing went further and committed itself to the ultimate aim of electing the Chief Executive and the entire legislature by universal suffrage.[2] Taken together, these commitments, if fulfilled, would distinguish Hong Kong both from its colonial past and from other cities in China.

The new era of empowering Hong Kong for autonomous rule, however, has turned out to be a reverse process of China taking full control. Critics point out that since the handover every Chief Executive of the SAR Government has been picked directly or indirectly by Beijing.[3] The civil service lost its decision-making power soon after 1997 and became the executive arm of political appointees trusted by Beijing.[4] The judiciary, nominally independent, has always accepted legal decisions related to Hong Kong, including interpretations of the Basic Law, from the Beijing-controlled Standing Committee of the National People's Congress (NPCSC). The plan for universal suffrage was

DOI: 10.4324/9781003150244-2

first delayed and then denied. Once having half of the seats elected by universal suffrage, the legislature has now been reconstituted with only 22% of the seats returned by direct elections – in which only Beijing-approved "patriots"[5] are allowed to run. "Hong Kong people ruling Hong Kong," once a catchphrase for democratic self-rule, became "patriots ruling Hong Kong." Beijing set up a second team to govern Hong Kong by pooling together Chinese officials from different departments responsible for Hong Kong affairs.[6] Coordinated by the Liaison Office of the Central People's Government in the Hong Kong SAR (LOCPG), this team helps govern Hong Kong by strengthening its influence operations, both covertly and overtly. It provides the narrative for political correctness and calls for action, maintains cohesion between pro-Beijing parties and organisations, builds grassroots networks for mass mobilisation, coordinates efforts to counter opposition initiatives, and helps run election campaigns for Beijing supporters.[7] This long arm of Beijing's sovereign power, together with the SAR Government, could in 2019 neither control nor contain the anti-Extradition Law Amendment Bill (ELAB) movement, which grew in popular support from a protest against an unpopular law to a mass campaign for universal suffrage and justice against police brutality.[8] China then took an alternative route to suppress the movement by cancelling OCTS. It ended the right to political freedoms and punished political opposition by enacting the National Security Law and imposing it on Hong Kong.[9] Since then, Hong Kong has become an autocratic state under the direct and indirect rule of China.[10]

Departing from the original design, Hong Kong's journey into autonomy was short-lived and its search for democracy prematurely ended. With the wisdom of hindsight, the early death of OCTS could be foretold by understanding two important facts: Beijing's own version of OCTS, which was markedly different from the Declaration, and the lack of checks and balances in the OCTS system as designed by the Declaration and the Basic Law. In short, China as Hong Kong's sovereign, according to Beijing's version, holds unlimited power beyond challenge over the SAR. It may determine and vary the limits of Hong Kong's autonomy, direct how it should be governed, and dictate who governs it.[11] China's unilateralism over Hong Kong hinges on the asymmetrical power relationship, provided by the Joint Declaration and the Basic Law, which leaves China unchecked to pursue its own version of OCTS even if it violates treaty obligations and constitutional bounds. We will first review the institutional fault line of OCTS before giving a historical account of why and how Beijing, in response to the governance crisis and political challenges, increased interference in the SAR after 1997. This in turn sowed the seeds of growing discontent and sometimes triggered confrontations between Beijing or Hong Kong authorities and Hong Kong people who took seriously the promise of democratic self-rule. It is only by understanding how conflicts recurred and crises deepened in the post-handover years that we can see how the OCTS experiment came to a premature close.

The systemic fault-line of "one country, two systems"

Constitutionally, the Hong Kong SAR was founded on the core concept – "a high degree of autonomy" – which divided power between the central and local governments. This constitutional concept was first expressed in the Sino-British Joint Declaration in 1984, which stipulates that Hong Kong "will enjoy a high degree of autonomy, except in foreign and defence affairs which are the responsibilities of the Central People's Government." It laid out the boundary between central and local governments by first spelling out what powers Beijing was to own over Hong Kong affairs, leaving the rest in the hands of the SAR Government.[12] But what matters most, in reality, is not only what powers the subsidiary government enjoys but also who owns the authority to define the scope of these powers.

China simply disregarded the original concept of self-rule and unilaterally changed it to an authoritarian version when it drafted the Basic Law. The formulation "all but foreign and defence affairs" is missing in the Basic Law. It has been replaced by the stipulation that China authorises the Hong Kong SAR "to exercise a high degree of autonomy and enjoy executive, legislative and independent judicial power."[13] The concept of authorisation means Beijing can dictate the terms of autonomy as it finds fit, even to the extent of taking back what had been given. It also affirms that Hong Kong will only get whatever powers Beijing allows the SAR to run the territory. Under the unitary state, as practised in China, there is no room for resistance by a subsidiary government against the direction and decision of the central government.

With the discretionary power of authorisation, Beijing curtailed the scope of Hong Kong's autonomy in four specific areas. First, the Basic Law puts restrictions on the SAR's fiscal policies. While the SAR can draw up its budget, it should keep "the expenditure within the limits of revenues" and ensure that "the budget is commensurate with the growth rate of its gross domestic product."[14] Second, it withholds the SAR's power to make economic and trade policies, which was clearly spelt out in the Joint Declaration, but is not in the Basic Law.[15] Third, the supervisory power of the legislature as a representative institution over the administration was weakened. Instead of providing for "comprehensive accountability" to the legislature for all matters the government is responsible for, the Basic Law confines the government's accountability to only four areas: implementing laws passed by the legislature and currently in force; presenting policy addresses to the Council; answering questions by Legislative Councillors; and obtaining the Council's approval for taxation and expenditure.[16] Last, the independence of the judiciary and the power of final adjudication by Hong Kong courts, as stated in the Joint Declaration, were compromised, as the Basic Law asserts the NPCSC's power to interpret the Basic Law's provisions.[17] As a result, Hong Kong courts have to follow NPCSC interpretations. From the administration to the legislature and the judiciary, the powers of all three branches of the SAR Government were watered down, long before 1997.

These inconsistencies with the Joint Declaration amounted to a breach of the international agreement. But Beijing's plan for Hong Kong encountered only feeble resistance. Aware of the divergence of the Basic Law from the Joint Declaration, the British Government expressed its disagreement only in confidential correspondence with China.[18] Publicly, it refrained from denouncing China's violation of the Sino-British agreement in the false hope that in private meetings Britain could better convince China to change its mind.[19] More fundamentally, the Joint Declaration, even though it was registered with the Secretariat of the United Nations,[20] had not been prepared to be legally binding. It named no authority to interpret the terms of the agreement. Neither did it provide a mechanism to handle disputes between the signing parties. Hong Kong people, once denied the right to join the negotiations over their own future, were again deprived of any role in safeguarding their interests in the implementation of the Joint Declaration.

Absent any mechanism of check and balance, the Joint Declaration is at best a gentleman's agreement, at worst a deficient contract the signing parties are free to depart from. China has simply taken advantage of this loophole in the Declaration. In the name of implementing the Joint Declaration, China installed a constitutional framework for Hong Kong based on its own conception of autonomy. Most important of all, it asserted that the power of amending the Basic Law is vested in the National People's Congress and the final authority of interpretation in the Standing Committee of the Congress. The ultimate control of the content and meaning of the Basic Law and in particular the autonomy of Hong Kong is firmly held in the hands of Beijing.[21] On the other hand, by failing to object publicly to China's violation of the letter and spirit of the Joint Declaration, Britain set a precedent for evading its moral, political, and legal responsibilities for Hong Kong. The original purpose of the Joint Declaration, to safeguard Hong Kong's autonomy after 1997, was thus betrayed.

Hands-off policy, political red line, and the rise of multiple interventions in Hong Kong

When the red line is crossed

China was widely seen as practising a hands-off policy in the formative years of the SAR.[22] The leadership of the SAR Government was made up of Hong Kong locals. They carried out all the duties of a sovereign government except in foreign affairs and defence matters. They were also solely responsible for making and executing plans for such policy areas as housing, education, and the elderly. Even amid serious challenges arising from economic recession, financial instability, or the public health crisis caused by the SARS epidemic,

Hong Kong was left to its own devices. The new sovereign and its representatives in Hong Kong played no active role in shaping its development. Hong Kong was still far from a democracy – its governing elites were selected or endorsed by Beijing – but it was a kind of self-rule without overt intervention from the sovereign. Overall, in the first five years after the handover, the British Government expressed its satisfaction in carefully chosen words that OCTS "generally works well in practice" as it found Hong Kong remained able "to exercise its autonomy in all matters envisaged under the Joint Declaration."[23]

What was not envisaged was that Beijing would step into Hong Kong affairs if it found a red line had been crossed. In 1999, after the Court of Final Appeal (CFA) ruled against the SAR Government in a right of abode case, the Chinese authorities, at the SAR Government's request, reversed the court's decision by interpreting the Basic Law.[24] The CFA's original decision affirmed the right of abode as a birthright for the offspring of Hong Kong people, wherever they were born. It invalidated the immigration rule by which children of Hong Kong permanent residents born in China had to obtain a one-way permit from the Chinese authorities to come to Hong Kong before the SAR Government could approve their applications for the right of abode in Hong Kong. The court also asserted its jurisdiction in reviewing the legislation made by the National People's Congress (NPC) or its Standing Committee (NPCSC) and voiding them if the court found that they were inconsistent with the Basic Law. The verdict triggered strong reactions from both Hong Kong and Chinese authorities. The SAR Government claimed it was impractical to follow the court's decision because as many as 1.67 million people, according to official estimates, would be entitled to the right of abode, and they could move from mainland China to Hong Kong. Beijing, on the other hand, objected to the CFA's assertion of power to overrule acts of the NPC or NPCSC. To China, it was not only disrespectful to the national legislature but was also *ultra vires* for the CFA to exercise the final authority in the SAR to interpret Chinese legislation, including the Basic Law. To counteract this, five months after the CFA's verdict, the NPCSC interpreted the relevant provisions of the Basic Law, endorsing the requirement of the one-way permit as a condition for obtaining the right of abode in Hong Kong. The judicial decision of the CFA, supposedly the final adjudication, was openly criticised and overturned by the Chinese authorities. The practice once deemed illegal was reinstated, and NPCSC's authority was thus restored.

In sharp contrast with the laissez-faire approach, this example of blatant intervention was the rare exception that proves the rule. In the initial years of the SAR, Beijing no doubt had kept its hands to itself, but only as long as it perceived no challenge to its power and authority. If Chinese leaders saw a potential threat to their supreme status in supervising Hong Kong, they would counteract to recover lost ground and reset the system to prevent future challenges. The 1999 interpretation of the Basic Law by NPCSC can be conceived as a measure not only to reverse Hong Kong's judicial decision but also to entrench Beijing's final authority over the Basic Law by defining the CFA as subordinate to the NPCSC.

What is wrong with the governance crisis?

The same consideration for intervention came into force again in the aftermath of the 2003 political crisis resulting from multiple failures in governance. Developed since 1997, these failures involved government ineptitude, inadequacy, or unresponsiveness in dealing with public issues such as economic hardship in recession years, the property-price crash, unpopular social reforms, public health threats from the SARS pandemic, and national security legislation.[25] They generated fierce public resentment against the administration and gradually evolved into a confidence crisis for the SAR Government. While failing to address outstanding social issues, the SAR Government planned to strengthen control of civil and political freedom by introducing national security legislation.[26] This spread the fear of state repression, fuelled political discontent, and transformed public frustration and anger into collective action on an unprecedented scale. Over half a million people took to the streets, demanding the deposition of Chief Executive Tung Chee-hwa and universal suffrage of both the Chief Executive and the legislature. With massive mobilisation in this campaign from all walks of life, and in particular professionals, more civic groups were formed, civil society was activated, and the opposition camp was empowered. A popular pro-democracy movement had come of age.

Eventually, the national security legislative process turned out to be a flop. The government failed to secure majority support for the bill after some pro-government legislators withdrew their blessing. The legislation was then called off. The government as well as the pro-Beijing camp in Hong Kong, which supported the national security legislation, had suffered an unmitigated defeat. The bill that would serve to protect national security was rejected by the public and shelved indefinitely. The patriotic cause was lost. Two top government officials resigned. Government popularity plunged to a historic low since 1997; 68.3% of those interviewed were dissatisfied with its performance.[27] With about half of the populace expressing distrust of the government, its legitimacy was called into question.[28] In the 2003 local elections, pro-government political parties experienced tremendous defeats. For instance, the largest pro-Beijing political party, the Democratic Alliance for the Betterment of Hong Kong (DAB), lost 25% of their seats, while its counterpart in the democratic camp, the Democratic Party (DP), gained 21%.[29]

The SAR Government was now close to complete failure. It had been incompetent in reviving a failing economy and had failed to address livelihood issues. It had been defeated in the patriotic cause of national security legislation, failing to secure cohesion and continued support from the pro-government camp. It lacked popular support and mass mobilisation to counteract the opposition camp. Disconnected from its people, it ruled without authority or efficacy.[30] This list of deficiencies aside, Beijing officials also noticed what they considered new developments in Hong Kong. The authorities were surprised that Hong Kong had transformed from a politically apathetic colony to a hotbed of revolt and dissension after 1997. They were also alarmed by the success of political organisations in Hong Kong that dared to criticise and confront Beijing, and mobilised mass support for their campaigns. Lastly, they were alerted to foreign influences in Hong Kong, including foreign nationals participating in the civil service, judiciary, protests, and elections, which might affect future developments. Recent changes had created a new political environment that, if unaddressed, might jeopardise Beijing's dominance over Hong Kong.[31] With these three concerns in mind, Beijing identified the pro-democracy camp and foreign influences as the major causes of political instability. To solve the problem a two-pronged strategy was in order: restrain and reduce, if not root out, the influence of the two sources of dissent and at the same time to strengthen the power and persuasive force of the SAR Government and its allies in governing Hong Kong.

The emergence of multiple interventions by China and the second governing team

Accordingly, Beijing worked on four fronts for the above strategic goals. On the constitutional front a halt was called to further democratisation in order to constrain the growth of the pro-democracy camp in popularity and influence through elections.[32] As shown in the first three Legislative Council elections after 1997, direct elections, by which 50% of Legislative Council seats were returned in 2004, favoured the pro-democracy camp. They took 60% of the directly elected seats in 2004, though the pro-Beijing camp continued to dominate in the legislature as the other seats were returned by undemocratic means. Any further increase in directly elected seats, not to say the introduction of universal suffrage as promised in the Basic Law, would worsen the situation.[33] Eventually, the pro-democracy camp would take the lead in the legislature unless Beijing stopped the process of democratisation in Hong Kong. Owning unchallengeable authority from the Basic Law, Beijing in the name of interpretation revised the law in its favour. The promised universal suffrage elections of the Chief Executive and the whole legislature in 2007 and 2008 respectively were postponed indefinitely. Preconditions for political reform were added, which required the SAR Government to obtain Beijing's approval both before starting the reform process and after reaching a decision in Hong Kong. The road to universal suffrage was blocked.[34]

On the political front, Beijing's local representatives started to appear in every corner of Hong Kong politics. They directed the leadership reshuffle of the ailing SAR Government, which was still run by the failing Chief Executive Tung Chee-hwa after the 2003 crisis and remained severely hit by undissipated public discontent and massive protests. Tung quit the job in March 2005 for health reasons after he was publicly criticised by China's President Hu Jintao. Beijing replaced him with a career civil servant, Donald Tsang, then the Chief Secretary for Administration, to cool the heat of public dissatisfaction. For the longer-term strategy, Beijing reshaped its united front work in Hong Kong, meaning efforts to increase influence over the SAR by winning friends and building alliances while isolating enemies. Beijing's first task was to deploy its most trusted followers or "patriots," mainly drawn from the pool of Hong Kong delegates to NPC and CPPCC, to various positions in the SAR Government, including principal officials and members of the Executive Council, the highest decision-making body. Some were assigned seats or even chairmanships in major government advisory and statutory committees. In the legislature, members of the NPC or CPPCC took a greater share of seats because more of them were elected and more elected legislators were recruited to these two national organs. Networks of officially endorsed "patriots" were thus formed in the political establishment through which Beijing exerted its influence over the governance of Hong Kong.[35]

Beijing also realised the urgent need to beef up support in civil society after the 2003 crisis. The strong leadership and solidarity of the middle class generally and professional groups in particular, as shown in the anti-government campaign, spoke volumes about the failure of the Beijing and SAR governments to win hearts and minds since the political handover. On the other hand, pro-Beijing networks of support, well-known for their skills in grassroots organisations and vote-canvassing in election campaigns, had failed to rally mass support to counter the rising opposition movement. Last but not least, the government-business alliance was unreliable. The withdrawal of political support for national security legislation by the Liberal Party, a political party representing business interests, had left the government with no choice but to abort the patriotic cause.

To recover lost ground, Beijing leaders reformed the united front strategy by fostering closer ties with business allies, expanding their sphere of influence among professionals, and strengthening mass organizations.[36] Since 2003, Beijing has appointed a greater number of business leaders and pro-government legislators as NPC or CPPCC members. With greater power and privilege comes closer supervision by Beijing, as both national power organs are under the leadership of the ruling Chinese Communist Party (CCP). Beijing was also keen to help groom the second generation of Hong Kong business tycoons to be future leaders by supporting the charitable organisations set up with the self-professed aim of promoting patriotic education among the youth and supporting the SAR Government. To increase influence over professionals, pro-Beijing professional associations, covering more than ten professions, were established in the aftermath of the 2003 crisis. They served as organisational networks to spread patriotism, recruit followers, and nurture pro-Beijing professional leaders. A pro-government base of local professionals, which was conspicuously absent before 2003, was established.

In strengthening mass organisations, Beijing stepped up efforts to build multi-layered and functional grassroots networks of political support. The first two types of networks, namely hometown associations and community organisations, not only grew in number after 2003 but were more organised through integration into a larger framework. While individual hometown associations targeted migrants from the same cities or counties in China, forming a layer of grassroots contacts, a superior layer of province-based federations of hometown associations was established. Each federation works to recruit hometown associations of localities within the province under its organisational umbrella.[37] For community organisations, three region-based federations were set up or activated in Hong Kong Island, Kowloon, and the New Territories. They gathered under one roof different types of community associations within the region, from youth and women's groups to neighbourhood organisations and mutual aid committees.[38] The third type of organisation was NGOs rendering tailor-made services to specific target groups. The New Home Association, for instance, provides a full range of services from information and counselling to job training for newly arrived Chinese immigrants and, later, ethnic minorities, to help them settle in Hong Kong. All these types of organisation were led and sponsored by pro-Beijing figures, well connected with local governments in China or China's Liaison Office in Hong Kong. Many of them, heavily funded by government money, professed the aim of supporting the SAR Government.[39] Together with traditional civic groups and trade unions controlled or co-opted by Beijing, they formed a multi-layered network, capturing organised support from various bases in civil society for the state.

Beijing also sought to beef up its ideological influence in Hong Kong. Its objectives included promoting patriotism, boosting national identity, and enhancing nationalistic education. Classroom teaching would feature China's greatness in its cultural heritage as well as general advancement since economic reforms, while skipping the dark side of Chinese history such as the Cultural Revolution and the Beijing massacre in 1989.[40] Outside the classroom, mainland exchange programmes were funded or organised by the SAR Government and pro-Beijing youth organisations. Participants in study tours, visits and internships, it was hoped, would gain a favourable view of the country.[41] In public discourse, the pro-Beijing media took the offensive to combat the pro-democracy narrative for universal suffrage in Hong Kong. They promoted a kind of patriotism which advocated the precedence of love and support of one's own country, or China, over democracy. And China, as Beijing conceived and publicised it, was the ruling CCP. This official narrative, that democracy without patriotism is prejudicial to China, formed the ideological basis for condemning pro-democracy leaders who campaigned for faster democratisation in Hong Kong.[42] By naming and blaming them as anti-China and unpatriotic, Beijing raised the alarm for supporters of the pro-democracy movement, with the intended effect of separating their leaders and organisations from followers. It also served to justify Beijing's later decision calling off the scheduled implementation of universal suffrage for the Chief Executive and the legislature. If this peculiar concept of patriotism was a precondition for further democratisation, universal suffrage receded into the distant future.

To further increase its influence, Beijing steered Hong Kong's economy towards greater dependence on China. Policies facilitated greater mobility of people, capital, and business across the border. Cross-border infrastructure projects were initiated to boost capacity for an increasing flow of visitors and goods.[43] Intergovernmental mechanisms were set up by the SAR Government and local governments in the Pearl River Delta Region to boost regional cooperation in common initiatives.[44] As a result, China enjoyed substantial growth in economic influence over Hong Kong. Mainland Chinese emerged to top the rank of both foreign visitors and investors in Hong Kong, while the mainland remained the largest trading partner for Hong Kong. In the financial market, Chinese enterprises became the leading group in Hong Kong's equity market in terms of both market capitalisation and turnover.[45] The long-term development of Hong Kong has been incorporated into Beijing's five-year economic plan since 2006, making it an integral part of China's economic blueprint. In the National 12th Five-Year Plan (2011–2015), for instance, Beijing defined Hong Kong's role as "an international centre for financial services, trade, and shipping" serving China's regional and economic development. It also assigned specific tasks for the SAR Government, such as running an offshore Renminbi centre, building cross-border infrastructure, and participating in regional cooperation in the Pearl River Delta region. And it affirmed Beijing's support to accomplish these prescribed initiatives.[46] Beijing is not only a dominant economic player but also the decision-maker directing the economic destiny of Hong Kong.

Powered by the absolute authority over the interpretation of the Basic Law, reinvigorated multi-layered networks of influence, policies of ideological indoctrination, and cross-border economic integration, Beijing struck back forcefully. Democratisation was arrested. The challenge of pro-democracy forces was contained. State power was injected into civil society to strengthen support for the government and pro-Beijing political parties. The younger generation was under Beijing's ideological influence through national education in schools and community activities. Together with growing economic dominance over Hong Kong and cross-border integration, Beijing was set to hold Hong Kong in a "tight embrace".[47] These strategic measures, however, demonstrated Beijing's crossing the boundary of Hong Kong's autonomy over its domestic affairs.

At the top echelon of power in Beijing, the Central Coordination Group for Hong Kong and Macao Affairs, formed and headed by a member of the Politburo standing committee of the ruling CCP,[48] would set policies and strategies as well as direct and coordinate operations by different departments responsible for Hong Kong affairs. On the ground in Hong Kong, the Liaison Office of the Central People's Government in the Hong Kong Special Administrative Region (LOCPG), the de facto Party Committee of Hong Kong, shifted to a proactive role in meddling with local politics.[49] It led the pro-Beijing camp, helped build the ruling alliance, dealt with business leaders, established rapport with professionals, supervised united front organisations, and through the official organs launched political attacks on opposition figures and parties. In elections, LOCPG was also a key player. It nurtured candidates, arbitrated conflicts between pro-government parties, mobilised voters' support, and ran smear campaigns against rival candidates. The office was also required to negotiate with the pro-democracy camp on the question of universal suffrage. The newly added tasks necessitated a huge expansion of LOCPG from a five-bureau office to a shadow government with more than twenty bureaus.[50] It is no exaggeration to remark, as a LOCPG official did, that, in addition to the SAR Government, the second governing team, formed by Chinese officials, had come of age.[51]

New tensions, strong resistance, and further repression

Growing dominance and stronger resistance

Beijing's blatant interference in Hong Kong, however, brought to life new tensions and strong resistance. The huge increase in mainland Chinese visitors, though beneficial to Hong Kong economically, also created social problems and conflicts. Urban spaces, public transport, recreation facilities, and resort places were overcrowded with the influx of mainland visitors. The phenomenal growth of parallel traders, especially in localities close to the border, turned community retail shops into busy wholesale markets for the favourite goods of mainland shoppers, such as infant formula and cigarettes.[52] In 2011, more than 35,000 mainland pregnant women took advantage of easy access to Hong Kong after 2003 and came to Hong Kong to give birth, mainly in public hospitals. This was conceived as an economical shortcut to obtaining permanent residency for their offspring.[53] These unwelcome developments created popular discontent and sparked off growing protest actions against the parallel traders and mainlanders' "invasion."

On the ideological front, while Hongkongers were reminded of their Chinese national identity by daily broadcasts of promotional videos with the national anthem before news programmes on TV,[54] prominent pro-democracy leaders and activists were condemned by Beijing's media in Hong Kong as unpatriotic or undesirable elements who "oppose China, disrupt Hong

Kong."[55] National education in schools, on the other hand, aimed to enhance the sense of belonging to China by presenting a biased view of China. At first, the curriculum soft sold Chinese cultural heritage and present-day achievements since economic reforms in the 1980s while sweeping under the carpet national tragedies such as the Great Leap Forward and the Cultural Revolution. Later on, national education shifted its focus to promoting brainwashing propaganda, including the assertion of the "Chinese model" and portraying the ruling party as "progressive, selfless, and united."[56] In 2012 a host of civil society organisations, led by student and parent groups, organised a week-long sit-in protest against national education in front of the Government headquarters. The Government was compelled to withdraw the programme when over 120,000 supporters showed up.[57]

Politically, Hongkongers grew disillusioned as they realised universal suffrage was not a matter of time as stipulated in the Basic Law but required Beijing's approval, which was unlikely to be given. Beijing's subsequent decisions, first to postpone universal suffrage to 2017 and later to add a patriotism requirement for Chief Executive candidacy, confirmed Beijing's denial of democracy in Hong Kong.[58] To seize back what had been lost, some pro-democracy leaders concluded, Hongkongers must think outside the box and act with collective resolve. Borrowing ideas from Mahatma Gandhi and Martin Luther King, one dominant view advocated the use of civil disobedience to press for change. This line of thought led to plans for a pro-democracy campaign, known as Occupy Central, a 10,000-strong peaceful sit-in protest to be held indefinitely on public roads in Central, Hong Kong's central business district. Planners hoped that mass support generated by the protestors' bravery and determination, along with the resulting chaos from the protest and the close scrutiny of the international media, would compel Beijing to yield and allow universal suffrage. The Occupy Central idea, though law-breaking, was widely supported by pro-democracy groups and put into practice at the end of September 2014, with sit-in protestors occupying major roads in three urban localities.[59]

China's tightening grip and the growth of Hong Kong identity

Unyielding to resistance and revolt, Beijing tightened its grip on Hong Kong. Before Occupy Central took place, Beijing positioned itself on the high ground of a sovereign owner in the White Paper on Hong Kong promulgated in June 2014. It asserted full jurisdiction over Hong Kong, thereby declaring Beijing's authority to dictate the terms of Hong Kong's autonomy and democracy, or the lack thereof. Any challenge to this authority represented a denial of Beijing's constitutional status and was thus illegitimate.[60] Later on in August, NPCSC made the decision to authorise a special kind of universal suffrage for the Chief Executive in 2017 which would allow "one-person, one-vote," while candidates for the elections were to be chosen by a Beijing-controlled Election Committee.[61] This proposal, if endorsed, would spell the end of the road to genuine universal suffrage and was met with strong resistance and opposition.[62] On the mass front, satellite organisations closely associated with the pro-Beijing camp in Hong Kong mushroomed, running public campaigns to counter the impact of mass mobilisation by Occupy Central. They opposed Occupy Central with similar techniques to those used by the pro-democracy camp, including signature campaigns, media advertisements, protest rallies, and processions.[63] Thugs were also hired to disrupt Occupy Central's activities through violence and to create fear among the public.[64] As public support faded with time, the mass movement lost steam and died down after 79 days. The hope for universal suffrage was dimmed, if not dashed.[65]

On the other hand, Beijing's measures to stiffen control over Hong Kong proved counterproductive. Beijing's increasing interference with Hong Kong eroded rather than enhanced the sense of national identity among Hong Kong people in relation to China. In a 2015 opinion poll, the proportion of respondents who identified themselves as Hongkongers more than doubled the 2008 figure, while the percentage of those identifying themselves as Chinese was halved.[66] The vision of OCTS was also in doubt. People who had lost confidence in OCTS exceeded those who remained confident, turning the figure of net confidence negative.[67] The younger generation, in particular, was most sceptical about Hong Kong's future, as 80% of interviewees aged between 18 and 29 in a 2016 poll expressed that they had no confidence in OCTS.[68] China's influence, though increasing and immense, stood out negatively. It appeared as an unstoppable leviathan that undermined Hong Kong's autonomy, obliterated its identity, derailed its democratisation, restrained its development, and created social conflicts.

Ironically, the increasing and forceful presence of China, which was intended to assert nationalism and rein in Hong Kong, fostered its antithesis, the rise and growth of localism.[69] Since the early 2010s, a host of citizen campaigns had emerged, ranging from protests against the influx of mainlanders, the demand for greater say over the China-Hong Kong relationship and the pursuit of universal suffrage as the safeguard against Beijing's interference, to the quest for self-determination and even independence after the Joint Declaration's 50-year lifespan expired in 2047. Taken together, they sought to defend and preserve Hong Kong's integrity, including its core values, institutions, interests, identity and heritage.[70] They were different in their appeals and actions but all shared the common idea of a threat from China to the values and causes they treasured.

China's rise in the world and the exercise of comprehensive jurisdiction over Hong Kong

The Chinese dream of national rejuvenation

While losing popularity and facing strong resistance in Hong Kong, China gained international prominence and national pride from its shining economic performance. In 2010, China overtook Japan as the world's second largest economy after scoring a close to 10% annualized growth in the decade after joining the World Trade Organization.[71] Concurrently, Beijing shifted its priority from the pursuit of economic advancement to the nationalistic call for building a strong nation, or the so-called "Chinese Dream of National Rejuvenation," with the sizeable ambition of setting up a new international order and securing greater national unity under the CCP leadership.[72]

China's increased assertiveness internationally and repressiveness at home due to its growing sense of national pride and perceived threats, were well demonstrated in its changed policy in Hong Kong after the 2000s. Presumably in fear of losing control of Hong Kong, the ruling CCP stressed in the report to its 2012 National Congress that, more than maintaining the SAR's long-term stability and prosperity, the basic objectives of its Hong Kong policy should include upholding China's core interests, i.e., its sovereignty, security, and its leadership in China.[73] This overwhelming concern for sovereignty and security transformed the concept of Hong Kong's autonomous powers, which, as commonly believed, had been fixed in the Basic Law and left to the full discretion of the Hong Kong authorities. Instead, Beijing's white paper on the "one country, two systems" policy asserted in 2014 that China, as the sovereign of Hong Kong, owned the undiluted authority of exercising "comprehensive jurisdiction" over Hong Kong. This meant that everything, ranging from Hong Kong's foreign affairs and defence matters to its domestic affairs and constitutional development, was under Beijing's command. The powers now enjoyed by the Hong Kong authorities were just delegated by the central authorities, and could be varied or even taken back by the delegator.[74]

This proclamation of unlimited power over Hong Kong served to set Beijing completely free from both domestic and international constraints. Domestically, as Beijing believed, the Central Government's right to supervise subsidiary local governments, was undiminished by the Basic Law provisions intended to check its interference with Hong Kong. Internationally, Beijing disowned the legal validity of the Sino-British Joint Declaration in regulating its power over Hong Kong. The Chinese Foreign Ministry, on the eve of the 20th anniversary of Hong Kong's return to China, declared that the Joint Declaration was only "a historical document" with no practical significance.[75] And foreign countries, including Britain, which criticised China's Hong Kong policy, would be denounced as interfering with China's domestic affairs.[76]

Freed from constitutional constraints and treaty obligations, and facing the challenge of localism rising in the post-Occupy Movement era, Beijing, which viewed the control and containment of political opposition as essential to defending China's core interests, was bound to play hardball in Hong Kong. The legal requirement for candidates of the Legislative Council elections to sign a declaration that they upheld the Basic Law and pledge allegiance to the Hong Kong Special Administrative Region, which in the past was seen as a mere formality, was turned into political screening by government officials in 2016. Candidates who failed to satisfy officials that they believed in China's sovereignty over Hong Kong would be disqualified from the election.[77] Six candidates regarded by officials as pro-independence localists were rejected.[78] In 2020, the number grew to 12.[79] Similarly, from 2016 onwards, after the NPCSC's interpretation of relevant provisions in the Basic Law, Legislative Council members elect must read out the oath of office, which was the same as the signed declaration, in full accord with the prescribed text, sincerely and solemnly. Any elected member judged to have failed the requirements for content and manner even before the NPCSC's interpretation, was not allowed to retake the oath and was unseated immediately.[80] Six opposition members elect were thus disqualified.[81] Further, an NPCSC decision in 2020 affirmed that the declaration and the oath should be construed as a precondition that legislators must comply with during their tenure or they would be disqualified immediately.[82] Following this decision, the SAR Government disqualified four incumbent pro-democracy legislators, accusing them of failing to uphold the Basic Law, including expressing an objection to the enactment of the National Security Law in Hong Kong.[83]

In civil society, pro-Beijing organisations carried on their role in Occupy Central as a counter-campaigner against pro-democracy causes through various forms of mobilisation, ranging from protests and processions to signature campaigns and thug attacks. The hardliner groups of the pro-Beijing camp, in particular, grew more prominent as it adopted a confrontational approach to pursue individual pro-democracy leaders, academics, student activists, and localist groups.[84] They marched in universities to denounce academics they found unacceptable and demanded their dismissal.[85] They disrupted pro-democracy forums[86] and besieged the office of a pro-democracy legislator.[87] They encircled anti-government protestors[88] and attacked journalists asking questions which might embarrass them.[89] On the other hand, they solicited donations and organised rallies to support policemen who were charged with assaulting activists during the Occupy Movement.[90] In the ideological arena, apart from supporting Beijing's version of "universal suffrage" that allowed only Beijing-approved "patriots" to stand for election, they parroted the official Chinese discourses such as "Beijing cracked down on the pro-democracy movement in 1989 by force in order to save the nation" but "no one died in Tiananmen Square."[91] They also ran smear campaigns against targeted groups and individuals, falsely accusing them of holding a disagreeable view or accepting foreign money.[92] These provocative efforts might contain the spread of opposition thinking but also contributed to an atmosphere of enmity and hate between pro-establishment and opposition camps, deepening divisions and leaving no room for communication and compromise.

Concurrent with Beijing's new policies of control and containment, restrictions on freedom of the press and expression increased dramatically after the early 2010s.[93] While Beijing's allies continued with economic take-overs and advertising boycotts to expand their influence over media, heightened political pressure was widely felt. A news portal, *The House News*, for instance, which supported Occupy Central, suddenly closed down, just a few months before the movement kicked off. The portal owner was reportedly "frightened" as he found Hong Kong overwhelmed by a 'white terror' atmosphere which brought unbearable pressure on him and his family.[94] In established media, prominent radio phone-in hosts critical of the Beijing and Hong Kong authorities were fired.[95] A senior editor of *Ming Pao* was sacked in 2016 after the newspaper published the Panama Papers, which showed how Hong Kong as an international financial hub served wealthy Chinese channelling money out of China.[96] Two years earlier, the chief editor of the same paper was almost chopped to death by two hired attackers, after Ming Pao, in collaboration with the International Consortium of Investigative Journalists, disclosed the offshore holdings of China's business and political elite.[97] On the book publishing front, the disappearance of five booksellers of the Causeway Bay Bookstore in late 2015, all of whom were later found detained in the Chinese mainland, spelt the end of Hong Kong as a centre outside China for publishing and selling books banned in China. The fact that one of them, Lee Bo, was arrested in Hong Kong by Chinese "special agents" and abducted to the Chinese mainland for detention, demonstrated China's ruthlessness in silencing voices they deemed "dangerous" by extra-legal means.[98] As a result of all these frustrations, the "banned books" market in Hong Kong withered, investigative reporting on China-related sensitive topics diminished, and opposition media, if surviving, were run under severe economic and political pressures. Hong Kong's global ranking in press freedom plummeted from 18th place in 2002 to 73rd place in 2017, marking a significant deterioration over a span of 15 years. However, the situation worsened even further, reaching an all-time low ranking of 148th in 2022 and 135th in 2024, after the enactment of the National Security Law in 2020.[99]

Towards the endgame of "one country, two systems"

In less than 20 years after 1997, Beijing succeeded in transforming itself from a hands-off sovereign to an overwhelming hegemon, dominating political, economic, and ideological developments in Hong Kong. Wielding unlimited power established by the principle of sovereignty and constitutionally entrenched by the final authority of the NPCSC (National People's Congress Standing Committee) in interpreting the Basic Law, the sovereign state guided judicial decisions, re-set the direction and pace of Hong Kong's constitutional development, and removed "unwanted" elected legislators.

In the short history of the SAR, Beijing never lacked tactics to regain supremacy but never tried engagement with the opposition camp, which represented the views of 60% of the populace, to address their concerns and sort out differences. The majority's concern about Hong Kong's high degree of autonomy being increasingly threatened was conceived as a legitimate cause for intervention, preservation of its unique identity as a lack of patriotism, and the popular demand for universal suffrage as separatism.[100] Public confidence in Beijing continued to decline throughout the 2010s.[101]

Economically, China's ambition to seek greater political control of Hong Kong was also engendered by its enormous stake in the economy. It became the biggest non-local investor in Hong Kong and the leading partner in Hong Kong's major economic sectors such as exports of goods and services, re-export, tourism and retail trade.[102] Publicly listed mainland enterprises also played a dominant role in Hong Kong's equity market, accounting for more than 60% of total market capitalisation and 70% of equity turnover in 2015.[103] China also mandated Hong Kong to set up the world's largest offshore centre for RMB trade settlement and liquidity pool.[104] In the development blueprint of the Guangdong-Hong Kong-Macau-Greater Bay Area launched in 2017, China assigned Hong Kong the special role of an international hub for financial, transportation and trading services.[105] The economic future of both China and Hong Kong was tied up, hinging on whether Hong Kong would successfully fit into China's economic blueprint, generate the desired regional synergy, and deliver the national mission. If this mission was too important to fail, Beijing must ensure that the SAR Government strictly obeyed its orders to follow the plan and cooperate with other cities in the Bay Area. Hence, an increase in control over Hong Kong's governance became necessary to act as a political guarantee for achieving the imperative of economic synergy. Moreover, two decades into the era of the SAR, Hong Kong's economic strength relative to China in terms of its GDP proportion had diminished substantially from 15.6% to less than 2.8% in 2017.[106] In other words, even if Hong Kong's economy was adversely affected by China's tightening grip on its autonomy, the impact on China in terms of GDP would be insignificant.

Facing China's assertion of supremacy, Hongkongers remained faithful to their core values and fought for what they had been promised in ways within the framework of the existing liberal legal system. The increasing and deepening interventions by Beijing after 2003, instead of frightening off pro-democracy activists and supporters, only awakened more Hongkongers, particularly the younger generation, to the fragility of Hong Kong's autonomy. The national security legislation in 2003, for instance, intended to be imposed on Hong Kong at a time of economic recession and public health crisis, triggered public anger and drew widespread opposition, which was peacefully and forcefully voiced through an anti-government mass movement. The repressive legislation was finally struck down. Hong Kong people realised in this rare success the importance and power of citizen participation, an organised civil society, and pro-democracy media in making a difference for Hong Kong. But Beijing also learnt a lesson. It beefed up its influence operations and strove to discourage the pro-democracy movement. Subsequent NPCSC decisions demonstrated Beijing's reluctance, if not refusal, to honour its promise of universal suffrage. To pro-democracy leaders and supporters, these moves, instead of dashing their hopes and causes, motivated them to look for a new strategy for the challenge of an uncertain political future. Eventually they carried on their fight for democracy by a civil disobedience campaign, Occupy Central, to pressurise Beijing for concessions. Although the campaign ended fruitless, China remained unable to impose on Hong Kong its 2014 proposal of universal suffrage with Chinese characteristics because it failed to secure enough support in the legislature. The promise of democracy was not delivered but also not gone.

Defeated, disillusioned, and divided, the pro-democracy movement after Occupy Central was at a low ebb, harmed by dissensions among different factions and growing repression by the SAR regime. The cause of democracy was submerged, but not lost. Five years later, the movement was revived and reinvigorated with unprecedented strength and solidarity after protests against the Extradiction Law Amendment Bill (ELAB) broke out in 2019. The movement was at first a single-issue mass campaign against ELAB, which would empower the Chief Executive to approve extradition of suspects arrested by Hong Kong authorities to China for legal enforcement.[107] Later, as the government repeatedly ignored million-people-strong demonstrations, rejected the popular request for an investigation into police brutality against protestors as witnessed by mass media and human rights organisations, and refused to withdraw the bill, it evolved into a people's movement. The government's intransigence was attributed to its unaccountability to the public due to its undemocratic nature. Accordingly, the ultimate solution lay in political transformation by introducing universal suffrage in the formation of the administration and the legislature.[108] As the quest for democracy was integrated as a major demand of the anti-ELAB movement, the pro-democracy movement was reborn with enhanced vigour powered by popular support and unity among different factions.[109] The pro-democracy camp's landslide victory in the district council elections of November 2019 further showed overwhelming support of the anti-ELAB movement by the populace.[110] This tremendous success in local elections, which engendered strong public pressure against the repressive government, encouraged them to take a similar step again in the forthcoming Legislative Council elections in 2020. By forming an election coalition to avoid internal rivalry, they aimed at winning a majority of seats in the legislature. If successful, they could control the legislature and pressure the government to pay heed to the demands of the anti-ELAB movement such as universal suffrage and investigation of police misconduct in suppressing protests.[111]

Not to be outdone, Beijing hit back with more ferocious repressive measures in the short term and the long term. Meanwhile the police continued the brutal oppression of street protests,[112] followed by arrests of more than 10,000 protesters[113] and the imposition of lockdown measures due to COVID-19 banned public gatherings and stopped all kinds of protest activities.[114] For the long term, Beijing's ultimate solution lay in depriving Hongkongers of any right to resistance. It was to deprive them of the legal right to opposition by criminalising political rights, and in particular, the rights to freedom of speech, assembly, and association. One major device was the Beijing-enacted National Security Law (NSL), which was imposed on Hong Kong in July 2020.[115] Since then, 47 pro-democracy candidates for the Legislative Council elections, who joined the election coalition mentioned above, were charged with conspiracy to subvert the state power.[116] *Apple Daily*, a pro-democracy newspaper, was forced to close after seven senior executives were arrested and accused of conspiring to "collude with a foreign government," a national security crime under NSL, for publishing articles calling for sanctions against China and Hong Kong by a foreign government.[117] The Hong Kong Alliance in Support of Patriotic Democratic Movements of China, which had run annual vigils since 1989 to commemorate the bloody suppression of pro-democracy protests in Tiananmen, came under pressure in 2021. All seven members of its executive committee were arrested and remanded on different NSL charges. Its website was removed, social media accounts closed down, and items on display in its June 4th museum seized, all by the authorities empowered by NSL. Eventually, the Alliance decided to dissolve in late September 2021.[118] With the demise of the Hong Kong Professional Teachers' Union,[119] the largest teacher union, and the Hong Kong Confederation of Trade Unions,[120] the only independent union coalition, the Alliance's collapse meant the authorities had removed the three biggest organisations in Hong Kong's civil society. Two years after the NSL came into force, it was estimated that about sixty organisations had dissolved.[121]

In order to stifle political criticisms not covered by NSL, the Hong Kong authorities revived the sedition offences inherited from the British colonial era, which were enacted in 1938 and unused since the 1970s. The United Nations Human Rights Committee condemned these offences as restraining the legitimate right of citizens to freedom of speech, and criticised the SAR Government for using them against unionists, journalists, activists, and common people who dared to express various sorts of criticisms or discontent about the government.[122] For instance, an activist planning to stage a protest against the Beijing Winter Olympics was found guilty of sedition and sentenced to nine months in jail.[123] Netizens who expressed discontent with anti-epidemic measures for COVID-19,[124] or posted banned political slogans such as "Liberate Hong Kong",[125] were arrested over sedition charges. A group of speech therapists who produced a series of children's picture books on sheep and wolves, metaphorically referring to Hongkongers and Beijing respectively, were charged with inciting hatred against the authorities.[126] They were convicted and jailed for 19 months. Two editors of *Stand News*, a pro-democracy online platform, were arrested over charges of publishing seditious materials for running articles highly critical of the government. They were remanded in custody for about a year before being released on bail, but the news platform ceased operations after the police action.[127] As of July 2023, more than 140 people had been arrested on NSL-related charges, with 94 of them facing formal charges. Additionally, 71 arrests were made for sedition charges, and 46 of those arrested had been prosecuted.[128] Legal sanctions aside, the fear instigated by the national security regime helped spread mounting political pressure, encouraging self-censorship in all walks of life.[129] Among its effects, the national security regime led to a lack of organisations willing to host commemorations for the Tiananmen Square massacre,[130] news media dropping political cartoon columns,[131] restrictions on publishing books covering "sensitive topics," limited availability of such books in bookstores,[132] libraries removing "sensitive" books,[133] classroom teachings toeing the "party line,"[134] more movies banned from public viewing,[135] and no labour groups daring to organise any public assembly on Labour Day.[136] In short, political opposition was silenced, freedom of expression muted, and civil society dismantled.[137]

The operation was a success but the historic experiment died

By enforcing the NSL and sedition offences, Beijing bulldozed the legal structure of protection for political activism in Hong Kong, a defining feature of OCTS, effectively terminating the anti-ELAB movement and dismantling the opposition camp.

The appeal and resilience of the democracy movement can also be attributed to another defining feature of OCTS, i.e., the partial democratisation of the legislature since 1997. Despite being a half-democracy at best, and having limited representativeness as a whole, the legislature officially conferred on the directly elected legislators the status and legitimacy of representatives of Hongkongers by virtue of the electoral support they received.

Despite being established by the liberal legal order and a semi-democratic system to protect Hong Kong from Chinese communist dictatorship, the firewall against state repression lasted less than half of the guaranteed 50-year period. By declaring the Joint Declaration a historical document and exercising full jurisdiction over Hong Kong, China simply smashed the firewall. The political space for China and pro-democracy Hongkongers to co-exist and compete evaporated. From now on, there are no political freedoms. Representative politics has been abolished and the competitive race for directly elected seats ended. Hongkongers' rights and powers of opposition and resistance have been uprooted. Beijing has now secured complete political control over the SAR, claiming total victory over its pro-democracy rivals. The whole operation is a success but the historic experiment of OCTS has died prematurely. And the rest is history.

Notes

1 The text of the Joint Declaration and a brief summary of it can be accessed at: https://researchbriefings.files.parliament.uk/documents/CBP-8616/CBP-8616 .pdf

2 See Articles 45 and 68, *The Basic Law of the Hong Kong Special Administrative Region of the People's Republic of China* (The Basic Law). The original version, promulgated in 1990, can be accessed at: https://www.refworld.org/docid /3ae6b53d0.html. The latest edition, with the newly amended Annexes I and II detailing the new methods of elections of the Chief Executive and members of the Legislative Council, accessed at: https://www.basiclaw.gov.hk/filemanager/ content/en/files/basiclawtext/basiclaw_full_text.pdf

3 Verna Yu: Beijing Completely Broke Their Promise on Hong Kong, Says Veteran Democrat Martin Lee, *Hong Kong Free Press*, 19 April 2020, accessed at: https:// hongkongfp.com/2020/04/19/exclusive-beijing-completely-broke-their-promise -on-hong-kong-says-veteran-democrat-martin-lee/

4 See chapter 1, *Consultation Document on Further Development of the Political Appointment System*, accessed at: https://www.cmab.gov.hk/images/pa_consultation_e.pdf

5 Annexes I and II, *supra* note 2.

6 Cao Erbao, Governing Forces in Hong Kong under the Condition of "One Country, Two Systems," *Xuexi Shibao*, 28 January 2008.

7 Sonny Shiu-Hing Lo, Steven Chung-Fun Hung, and Jeff Hai-Chi Loo, *China's New United Front Work in Hong Kong: Penetrative Politics and Its Implications*, Singapore: Palgrave Macmillan, 2019.

8 Nam Kiu Tsing, *Hongkongers' Fight for Freedom: Voices from the 2019 Anti-Extradition Movement*, Leiden; Boston: Brill, 2023.

9 Amnesty International, Hong Kong's National Security Law: 10 Things You Need to Know, July 17 2020 accessed at: https://www.amnesty.org/en/latest/news /2020/07/hong-kong-national-security-law-10-things-you-need-to-know/

10 An assessment of the impact of the National Security Law on Hong Kong's rule of law can be found in 2022 Special Issue: Hong Kong's Changing Rule of Law, *Academia Sinica Law Journal*, May 2022, accessed at: https://www.iias.sinica .edu.tw/en/publication_post/1379/9

11 For an insider's view, see Jie Cheng, The Story of a New Policy, *Hong Kong Journal*, 7 January 2009 accessed at: http://www.hkbasiclaw.com/Hong%20Kong %20Journal/Cheng%20Jie%20article.htm

12 *Supra* note 1.

13 *Supra* note 2.

14 Article, The Basic Law, *supra* note 2. For an analysis of the differences between the Joint Declaration and the Basic Law, see Yiu Yeuk Wah, Wrestling in Black and White: How the Basic Law Deviates from the Joint Declaration, accessed at: https://medium.com/decoding-hong-kongs-history/%E7%99%BD%E7%B4%99 %E9%BB%91%E5%AD%97%E7%9A%84%E8%A7%92%E5%8A%9B-%E5 %9F%BA%E6%9C%AC%E6%B3%95-%E5%A6%82%E4%BD%95%E5%81 %8F%E9%9B%A2-%E4%B8%AD%E8%8B%B1%E8%81%AF%E5%90%88 %E8%81%B2%E6%98%8E-16f8d06216ce

15 Section VI of Annex I, Sino-British Joint Declaration Article, The Basic Law, *supra* note 2, *supra* note 1.

16 Article 64, The Basic Law, *supra* note 2.

17 Article 158, The Basic Law, *supra* note 2.

18 See Wrestling in Black and White: How the Basic Law Deviates from the Joint Declaration, *supra* note 14.

19 Ibid.
20 https://treaties.un.org/Pages/showDetails.aspx?objid=08000002800d4d6e
21 Articles 158 and 159, The Basic Law, *supra* note 2. See also Brian Z. Tamanaha, Post-1997 Hong Kong: A Comparative Study of the Meaning of "High Degree of Autonomy," *California Western International Law Journal*, 20(1) [1989], 41–66.
22 *Supra* note 11.
23 *Six-Monthly Report on Hong Kong (January–June 2002), Presented to Parliament by the Secretary of State for Foreign and Commonwealth Affairs by Command of Her Majesty*, July 2002, 1.
24 For an analysis of the legal conflict, see the following articles: Karmen Kam, Right of Abode Cases: The Judicial Independence of the Hong Kong Special Administrative Region v. The Sovereignty Interests of China, *Brook. J. Int'l L.*, 27(2), 611, 2002; Anne R. Fokstuen, The Right of Abode Cases: Hong Kong's Constitutional Crisis, *Hastings Int'l & Comp. L. Rev.*, 26(2), 265, 2003; and Johannes Chan, Judicial Independence: Controversies on the Constitutional Jurisdiction of the Court of Final Appeal of the Hong Kong Special Administrative Region, *Int'l L.*, 33(4) 1015, 1999.
25 For analyses of the 2003 governance crisis, see the following contributions: Hin Yeung Chan, *The Politics of Crisis Management in Post-1997 Hong Kong: a State-Society Interactive Framework*, a Phd thesis, Lingnan University 2014; Tai Lok Lui and Wing Kai Stephen Chiu, Governance Crisis in Post-1997 Hong Kong: A Political Economy Perspective, *China Review*, 7(2), 1–34, 2007; and Anthony B. L. Cheung, Hong Kong's Post-1997 Institutional Crisis: Problems of Governance and Institutional Incompatibility, *Journal of East Asian Studies*, 5(1), 135–167, January–April 2005.
26 For a brief introduction, see Albert H. Y. Chen, Hong Kong's Political Crisis of July 2003, *Hong Kong L.J.*, 33-2 265, 2003. A detailed discussion of various dimensions of the national security legislation can be found in Fu Hualing, Carole J. Petersen, and Simon N. M. Young (eds.) *National Security and Fundamental Freedoms: Hong Kong's Article 23 Under Scrutiny*, Hong Kong: Hong Kong University Press, 2005.
27 Hong Kong Public Opinion Research Institute, People's Satisfaction with the HKSAR Government 7/1997-6/2023, accessed at: https://www.pori.hk/pop-poll /government-en/h001.html?lang=en
28 Hong Kong Public Opinion Research Institute, People's Trust in the HKSAR Government, 9/1992-5/2023, accessed at: https://www.pori.hk/pop-poll/govern-ment-en/k001.html?lang=en
29 Basic information can be found at 2003 Hong Kong Local Elections, Wikipedia, accessed at: https://en.wikipedia.org/wiki/2003_Hong_Kong_local_elections. For analysis, see Joseph Y. S. Cheng, The 2003 District Council Elections in Hong Kong, *Asian Survey*, 44(5), 734–754, 2004.
30 Ming Sing, *Politics and Government in Hong Kong: Crisis under Chinese Sovereignty*, London and New York: Routledge, 2009.
31 *Supra* note 11.
32 An account on Hong Kong's democratisation in the first decade after 1997 is provided by Ma Ngok, Democratic Development in Hong Kong: A Decade of Lost Opportunities, in *The Hong Kong Special Administrative Region in Its First Decade*, Joseph Y. S. Cheng (ed.), Hong Kong: City University of Hong Kong Press, 49–74, 2007. For discussion of the constitutional development of democ-racy, see: Michael C. Davis, The Basic Law and Democratisation in Hong Kong, *Loy. U. Chi. Int'l L. Rev.*, 3, 165, 2006, accessed at: http://lawcommons.luc.edu/ lucilr/vol3/iss2/5

33 Basic information on the electoral support received by different political parties is provided by Chung Fun Steven Hung, Reviewing and Evaluating the Direct Elections to the Legislative Council and the Transformation of Political Parties in Hong Kong, 1991–2016, *Journal of US-China Public Administration*, 13(8), 499–517, 2016.

34 A detailed analysis of the said interpretation of the Basic Law is provided by Ricky Y. H. Fong, Universal Suffrage in Hong Kong: Promise or Illusion? A Critical Analysis of National People's Congress Standing Committee's Interpretation of Hong Kong Basic Law Annexes, *UCLA Pacific Basin Law Journal*, 24, 225, 2007, accessed at: https://escholarship.org/uc/item/9cp3s58z

35 Peter T. Y. Cheung, The Changing Relations between Hong Kong and the Mainland since 2003, in Wai-man Lam, Percy Luen-tim Lui, and Wilson Wong (eds.), *Contemporary Hong Kong Government and Politics*, Hong Kong: Hong Kong University Press, 2012, 325–348.

36 Ibid. Other studies on various dimensions of the united fronts in Hong Kong are helpful in understanding its operations, including the following: Lo, Hung and Loo (2019), *supra* note 7; Edmund W. Cheng, United Front Work and Mechanism of Countermobilization in Hong Kong, *The China Journal*, 83, 1–33, 2020; Wai-man Lam, China's Changing Ruling Strategies on Hong Kong and Their Implications, *Contemporary Chinese Political Economy and Strategic Relations: An International Journal* 6(3), 953–992, 2020; Yuen and Edmund W. Cheng, Deepening the State: The Dynamics of China's United Front Work in Post-Handover Hong Kong, *Communist and Post-Communist Studies*, 53(4), 136–154, 2021; Eliza W. Y. Lee, United Front, Clientelism, and Indirect Rule: Theorizing the Role of the "Liaison Office" in Hong Kong, *Journal of Contemporary China*, 29(125), 763–775, 2020.

37 Cheng (2020), 9; Yuen and Cheng (2021), 144, see note above.

38 Cheng (2020), 10, Yuen and Cheng (2021), 145, see note above.

39 Cheng (2020), 11, Yuen and Cheng (2021), 145–146, see note above.

40 Controversies in national education are discussed in: Yan Wing Leung, Nationalistic Education and Indoctrination, *Citizenship, Social and Economics Education*, 116–130, 2004; Yan Wing Leung, Understandings and Teaching Approaches in Nationalistic Education: The Case of Hong Kong, *Pacific-Asian Education*, 19(1), 72–89, 2007; George Siu-Keung Ngai, Yan Wing Leung, and Timothy Wai-Wa Yuen, The Turmoil about Efforts to Implement National Education in Hong Kong: An Overview and Analysis, *The Social Educator*, 32(1), 5–15, 2014; Paul Morris and Edward Vickers, Schooling, Politics and the Construction of Identity in Hong Kong: The 2012 "Moral and National Education" Crisis in Historical Context, *Comparative Education*, 51(3), 305–326, 2015; Kan, K., "Lessons in Patriotism: Producing National Subjects and the De Sinicisation Debate in China's Post-Colonial City, *China Perspectives*, 4, 63–69, 2012.

41 *Supra* note 35.

42 Articles on both sides of the controversy are collected in an anthology titled *The Patriotism Debate*, Ming Pao, 2004.

43 *Supra* note 35.

44 Peter T. Y. Cheung, Intergovernmental Relations between Mainland China and the Hong Kong SAR, in Evan M. Berman (ed.), *Public Administration in Southeast Asia: Thailand, Philippines, Malaysia, Hong Kong and Macao*, Florida: CRC Press, 2011, 255–281.

45 *Supra* note 35.

46 The full text of the report and the summary of relevant content on Hong Kong by the SAR Government (The HKSAR's Work in Complementing the National 12th Five-Year Plan) can be accessed at: https://www.cmab.gov.hk/en/issues/12th

_5yrsplan.htm. For a brief discussion on Hong Kong as the offshore centre for Renminbi, see Edmund Ho, Role of Hong Kong as a RMB Offshore Centre, Hong Kong Sustainable Development Research Institute, October 2012.

47 *Supra* note 35.

48 The Group was renamed as Central Leading Group on Hong Kong and Macau Affairs in 2020.

49 *Supra* note 36.

50 Cheng (2020), *supra* note 36.

51 *Supra* note 6.

52 Peter T. Y. Cheung, In Beijing's Tightening Grip: Changing Mainland-Hong Kong Relations amid Integration and Confrontation, in Brian C. H. Fong and Tai-lok Lui (eds.), *Hong Kong 20 Years after the Handover: Emerging Social and Institutional Fractures after 1997*, Basingstoke: Palgrave Macmillan, 2018, 255–286.

53 Ibid.

54 https://www.info.gov.hk/gia/general/200410/13/1013173.htm

55 *Supra* note 42. A specialised study on the use of metaphors in the patriotism debate by two ideologically opposing newspapers is helpful in understanding how Beijing views the pro-democracy politicians in Hong Kong. See: John Flowerdew and Solomon Leong, Metaphors in the Discursive Construction of Patriotism: The Case of Hong Kong's Constitutional Reform Debate, *Discourse & Society*, 18(3), 273–294, May 2007.

56 See The Curriculum Development Council, Moral and National Education Curriculum Guide (Primary 1 to Secondary 6) Consultation Draft, May 2011, accessed at: https://www.legco.gov.hk/yr10-11/english/panels/ed/papers/ ed0509cb2-1748-2-e.pdf; Legislative Council Panel on Education Moral and National Education Curriculum, accessed at: https://www.legco.gov.hk/yr10-11 /english/panels/ed/papers/ed0627cb2-2172-1-e.pdf; and Tony Cheung, A History of How National Education Was Introduced in Hong Kong, *South China Morning Post*, 9 September 2012; Worldwide Reports on Anti-National Education Protest, (Chinese), accessed at: http://goo.gl/n2wih; Alexis Lai, "National Education" Raises Furor in Hong Kong, CNN, accessed at: http://edition.cnn.com/2012/07 /30/world/asia/hong-kong-national-education-controversy; National Education Service Centre, 中國模式――國情專題教學手冊 (*China Model National Conditions Teaching Manual*), Hong Kong: NESC, 2012, accessed at: https:// www.slideshare.net/WangHaoZhong/ss-14252905

57 Keith Bradsher, Hong Kong Retreats on "National Education" Plan, *New York Times*, 8 September 2012, accessed at: https://www.nytimes.com/2012/09/09 /world/asia/amid-protest-hong-kong-backs-down-on-moral-education-plan .html

58 Albert H. Y. Chen, The Law and Politics of the Struggle for Universal Suffrage in Hong Kong, 2013–15, *Asian Journal of Law and Society*, 3, 189–207, 2016, accessed at: https://web.archive.org/web/20190429083530id_/https://www .cambridge.org/core/services/aop-cambridge-core/content/view/1625110D441 4586604211E0B3CDC1312/S2052901515000212a.pdf/div-class-title-the-law -and-politics-of-the-struggle-for-universal-suffrage-in-hong-kong-2013-15-div .pdf

59 Reuters, Explainer: What Was Hong Kong's "Occupy" Movement All About?, April 24 2019, accessed at: https://www.reuters.com/article/us-hongkong-politics -occupy-explainer-idUSKCN1S005M; Raymond Lee, Hong Kong's Umbrella Movement, Al Jazeera Centre for Studies, 11 November 2014, accessed at: https:// studies.aljazeera.net/en/reports/2014/11/201411119524559672.html; Karita Kan, Occupy Central and Constitutional Reform in Hong Kong, *China Perspectives*,

3, 73–78, 2013; N. Ma and E. W. Cheng (eds.), *The Umbrella Movement: Civil Resistance and Contentious Space in Hong Kong*, Amsterdam: Amsterdam University Press, 2019. For a brief discussion, see Antony Dapiran, *A City of Protest: A Recent History of Dissent in Hong Kong*, Victoria: Penguin, 2017.

60 Information Office of the State Council, The People's Republic of China (June 2014), The Practice of the "One Country, Two Systems" Policy in the Hong Kong Special Administrative Region, accessed at: http://english.www.gov.cn/archive /white_paper/2014/08/23/content_281474982986578.htm; Kristie Lu Stout, Alarm in Hong Kong at Chinese White Paper Affirming Beijing Control, CNN, 13 June 2014. Accessed at https://www.youtube.com/watch?v=izK-xDLmQoM.

61 The Decision of the Standing Committee of the National People's Congress on Issues Relating to the Selection of the Chief Executive of the Hong Kong Special Administrative Region by Universal Suffrage and on the Method for Forming the Legislative Council of the Hong Kong Special Administrative Region in the Year 2016, accessed at: http://www.china.org.cn/china/2014-08/31/content_33390388 .htm; For the official explanation for the decision, see Li Fei, Explanations on the Draft Decision of the Standing Committee of the National People's Congress on Issues Relating to the Selection of the Chief Executive of the Hong Kong Special Administrative Region by Universal Suffrage and on the Method for Forming the Legislative Council of the Hong Kong Special Administrative Region in the Year 2016, accessed at:http://www.2017.gov.hk/filemanager/template/en/doc /20140827a.pdf

62 Richard C. Bush, China's Decision on Universal Suffrage in Hong Kong, Brookings Institution, 2 September 2014, accessed at: https://www.brookings.edu /articles/chinas-decision-on-universal-suffrage-in-hong-kong/; Michael Davis, The Basic Law, Universal Suffrage and the Rule of Law in Hong Kong, *Hastings Int'l & Comp. L. Rev.*, 38(275), 2015; Albert H. Y. Chen, *supra* note 58.

63 Cheng (2020); Lam (2020); Yuen and Cheng (2021), *supra* note 36.

64 Cheng (2020), *supra* note 36.

65 A detailed analysis of China's failure to deliver universal suffrage to Hong Kong is offered by Alvin Y. H. Cheung, Road to Nowhere: Hong Kong's Democratisation and China's Obligations Under Public International Law, *Brook. J. Int'l L.*, (40) 465, 2015, accessed at: http://brooklynworks.brooklaw.edu/bjil/vol40/iss2/3

66 Cheung (2018), *supra* note 52, 270.

67 Ibid.

68 Ibid.

69 Malte Philipp Kaeding, The Rise of "Localism" in Hong Kong, *Journal of Democracy*, 28(1), 158–171, 2017; Sebastian Veg, The Rise of "Localism" and Civic Identity in Post-Handover Hong Kong: Questioning the Chinese Nation-State, *The China Quarterly*, 230, 323–347, 2017, Samson Yuen and Sanho Chung, Explaining Localism in Post-Handover Hong Kong: An Eventful Approach *China Perspectives*, 3, 19–29, 2018; Yew Chiew Ping and Kwong Kin-ming, Hong Kong Identity on the Rise, *Asian Survey*, 54(6), 1088–1112, November/ December 2014.

70 Stephen Robert Nagy, Social Inequality and the Rise of Localism in Hong Kong, *International Studies Review,* 16(2), 25–47, December 2016; Ying-ho Kwong, The Growth of "Localism" in Hong Kong; a New Path for the Democracy Movement? *China Perspectives*, 3, 63–68, 2016; Stan Hok-Wui Wong and Kin Man Wan, The Housing Boom and the Rise of Localism in Hong Kong: Evidence from the Legislative Council Election in 2016, *China Perspectives*, 3, 31–40, 2018; Alvin So and Ping Lam Ip Civic Localism, Anti-Mainland Localism, and Independence: The Changing Pattern of Identity Politics in Hong Kong Special Administrative Region, *Asian Education and Development Studies*, March

2020, accessed at: https://www.researchgate.net/profile/Alvin-So/publication/342158586_Civic_localism_anti-mainland_localism_and_independence_The_changing_pattern_of_identity_politics_in_Hong_Kong_Special_Administrative_Region/links/5ee5a45492851ce9e7e38709/Civic-localism-anti-mainland-localism-and-independence-The-changing-pattern-of-identity-politics-in-Hong-Kong-Special-Administrative-Region.pdf; G. Lin, CUHK Survey Finds 40% of Young Hongkongers Want Independence after 2047, *Hong Kong Free Press*, July 25 2016, accessed at: www.hongkongfp.com/2016/07/25/17-hongkongerssupport-independence-2047-especially-youth-cuhk-survery/

71   Justin Paul, The Rise of China: What, When, Where, and Why?, *The International Trade Journal*, 1–16, March 2016. Economic figures used here are taken from the website of World Bank's Development Data Group, accessed at: https://data.worldbank.org/country/china

72   Zheng Wang, The Chinese Dream: Concept and Context, *Journal of Chinese Political Science*, 19, 1–13, 2014; Ming Wan, Xi Jinping's "China Dream": Same Bed, Different Dreams?, *Asan Forum*, August 2013, accessed at: file:///C:/Users/user/Downloads/Article-2013-Chinadream.pdf; William A. Callahan, China 2035: From the China Dream to the World Dream, *Global Affairs*, 1–13, 20 August 2016; Randall L. Schweller and Xiaoyu Pu, After Unipolarity: China's Visions of International Order in an Era of U.S. Decline, *International Security*, 36(1), 41–72, 2011.

73   Hu Jintao, *Firmly March on the Path of Socialism with Chinese Characteristics and Strive to Complete the Building of a Moderately Prosperous Society in All Respects*, Report to the Eighteenth National Congress of the Communist Party of China on 8 November 8 2012, accessed at: http://np.china-embassy.gov.cn/eng/Diplomacy/201211/t20121118_1586373.htm

74   Information Office of the State Council, The People's Republic of China (June 2014), *supra* note 60.

75   Reuters, China Says Sino-British Joint Declaration on Hong Kong No Longer Has Meaning, 30 June 2017, accessed at: https://www.reuters.com/article/us-hongkong-anniversary-china-idUSKBN19L1J1

76   Foreign Ministry Spokesperson Lu Kang's Regular Press Conference on 18 July 2019, accessed at: http://us.china-embassy.gov.cn/eng/fyrth/201907/t20190718_4473860.htm

77   EAC's Request to Sign Confirmation Form Has Legal Basis, Government Information & Services, accessed at: https://www.info.gov.hk/gia/general/201607/19/P2016071900950p.htm and the press release by the SAR Government: HKSAR Government Responds to Media Enquiries Regarding 2016 Legislative Council Election, accessed at: https://www.info.gov.hk/gia/general/201607/30/P2016073000700.htm

78   Rishi Iyengar, Hong Kong Is Banning Pro-Independence Candidates From Running in Elections, *Time Magazine*, 2 August 2016, accessed at: https://time.com/4436253/hong-kong-election-briefing-protests-edward-leung-china-independence/

79   Lucas Niewenhuis, Hong Kong Disqualifies a Dozen Pro-Democracy Candidates from Running for Office, *The China Project*, 30 July 2020, accessed at: https://thechinaproject.com/2020/07/30/hong-kong-disqualifies-a-dozen-pro-democracy-candidates-from-running-for-office/

80   Interpretation of Article 104 of the Basic Law of the Hong Kong Special Administrative Region of the People's Republic of China by the Standing Committee of the National People's Congress, 7 November 2016, accessed at: https://www.elegislation.gov.hk/hk/A115!en.assist.pdf

81 Kevin Lui, Four More Hong Kong Lawmakers Ousted in a Blow to Democratic Hopes, *Time Magazine*, 14 July 2017, accessed at: https://time.com/4856181/hong-kong-lawmakers-oath-china-disqualified/

82 "全国人民代表大会常务委员会关于香港特别行政区立法会议员资格问题的决定", (A Decision on the Qualifications for Members of the Hong Kong Legislative Council of the Hong Kong Special Administrative Region by the Standing Committee of the National People's Congress), accessed at: http://www.xinhuanet.com/politics/2020-11/11/c_1126725802.htm

83 Changhao Wei, NPCSC Clarifies "Allegiance" Requirements for Hong Kong Legislators, Disqualifies Pro-Democracy Legislators, *NPC Observer*, accessed at: https://npcobserver.com/2020/11/11/npcsc-clarifies-allegiance-requirements-for-hong-kong-legislators-disqualifies-pro-democracy-legislators/#:~:text=The%20NPC%20Standing%20Committee%20

84 Cheng (2020), *supra* note 36.

85 "傅振中入港大狙擊鍾庭耀 批民研收美國組織資助做假民調," *Standnews*, 29 August 2018, accessed at: https://web.archive.org/web/20190818073425/https://thestandnews.com/politics/%E5%82%85%E6%8C%AF%E4%B8%AD%E5%85%A5%E6%B8%AF%E5%A4%A7%E7%8B%99%E6%93%8A%E9%8D%BE%E5%BA%AD%E8%80%80-%E6%89%B9%E6%B0%91%E7%A0%94%E6%94%B6%E7%BE%8E%E5%9C%8B%E7%B5%84%E7%B9%94%E8%B3%87%E5%8A%A9%E5%81%9A%E5%81%87%E6%B0%91%E8%AA%BF/

86 Scott Neuman, Hong Kong Protesters Call Off Talks after Mobs Attack Their Camps, WBUR, 3 October 2014, accessed at: https://www.wbur.org/npr/353454741/anti-protest-mob-attacks-hong-kong-student-camp

87 "愛港力向「李卓人」掟蛋," *Oriental Daily*, 15 December 2013, accessed at: https://web.archive.org/web/20191028121646/https://orientaldaily.on.cc/cnt/news/20131215/00176_028.html

88 Lily Kuo and Heather Timmons, Pro-Beijing Groups Are Systematically Attacking Protests in Hong Kong, *Quartz*, 3 October 2014, accessed at: https://qz.com/275562/anti-occupiers-are-tearing-down-protesters-tents-in-hong-kong

89 Clare Jim, Anti-Occupy Mob Roughs up Hong Kong Journalists, Reuters, 26 October 2014, accessed at: https://www.reuters.com/article/us-hongkong-china-idUSKCN0IE0SL20141025; "挺梁遊行惹火 記者捱捧 沿途四爆衝突 愛港力劃清界線," 明報, 31 December 2012, accessed at: https://archive.ph/20130427043619/http://news.hk.msn.com/highlight/article.aspx#selection-703.5-703.16

90 "七警案撐警遊行罵法官 港律政司跟進," *Lianhe Zaobao*, 19 February 2017, accessed at: https://www.zaobao.com.sg/wencui/politic/story20170219-726639

91 "愛港之聲: 六四天安門廣場內無人死," *Bastile Post*, 28 May 2014, accessed at: https://www.bastillepost.com/hongkong/article/208783-%e6%84%9b%e6%b8%af%e4%b9%8b%e8%81%b2%ef%bc%9a%e5%85%ad%e5%9b%9b%e5%a4%a9%e5%ae%89%e9%96%80%e5%bb%a3%e5%a0%b4%e5%85%a7%e7%84%a1%e4%ba%ba%e6%ad%bb/

92 "愛護香港力量," 香港網絡大典, accessed at:https://evchk.fandom.com/zh/wiki/%E6%84%9B%E8%AD%B7%E9%A6%99%E6%B8%AF%E5%8A%9B%E9%87%8F#cite_note-13; *supra* note 96.

93 The following article lists 68 incidents related to censorship of expression since the Umbrella Movement to November 2018: Kong Tsung-gan, Censorship in Hong Kong since the Umbrella Movement: An Overview, *Medium*, 18 November 2018, accessed at: https://kongtsunggan.medium.com/censorship-in-hong-kong-since-the-umbrella-movement-an-overview-8024fdad68fc

94 "蔡東豪: 各位, 主場新聞今天要結束了！" 香港獨立媒體, 26 July 2014, accessed at: https://www.inmediahk.net/%E5%AA%92%E9%AB%94/%E8%94%A1%E6%9D%B1%E8%B1%AA%EF%BC%9A%E5%90%84%E4%BD%8D

%EF%BC%8C%E4%B8%BB%E5%A0%B4%E6%96%B0%E8%81%9E%E4
%BB%8A%E5%A4%A9%E8%A6%81%E7%B5%90%E6%9D%9F%E4%BA
%86%EF%BC%81

95 Francis L. F. Lee, Opinion Media: From Talk Radio to Internet Alternative
Websites, in Tai-lok Lui, Stephen W. K. Chui, and Ray Yep (eds.), *Routledge
Handbook of Contemporary Hong Kong*, London: Routledge, 2019, 170–184.
Also available at: https://books.google.com.tw/books?id=vDVlDwAAQBAJ&pg
=PT239&lpg=PT239&dq=Lee+Wai+Ling+fired+by+commercial+radio&source
=bl&ots=T2XCOrlq-t&sig=ACfU3U2FICCNkzVNWI_bNlVCLO-j1FeudA&hl
=en&sa=X&ved=2ahUKEwjAu9SRzfz_AhV8t1YBHQA0BEQQ6AF6BAge
EAM#v=onepage&q=Lee%20Wai%20Ling%20fired%20by%20commercial%
20radio&f=false

96 桑普，"解僱安裕與明報之觴，" Yahoo新聞, 23 April 2016, accessed at: https://tw
.news.yahoo.com/-030112812.html

97 International Consortium of Investigative Journalists, Leaked Records Reveal
Offshore Holdings of China's Elite. Files Shed Light on Nearly 22,000 Tax Haven
Clients from Hong Kong and Mainland China, 21 January 2014, accessed at:
https://www.icij.org/investigations/offshore/leaked-records-reveal-offshore-hold-
ings-of-chinas-elite/

98 Frank Langfitt, The Plot Thickens in the Mystery of Hong Kong's Missing
Booksellers, NPR, 5 January 2016, accessed at: https://www.npr.org/sections/par-
allels/2016/01/05/461997704/the-plot-thickens-in-the-mystery-of-hong-kongs
-missing-booksellers; A former Chinese spy, who later escaped to Australia, told
the BBC that Chinese spies were involved in the abduction of Lee Bo to China.
See "王立強：自稱是間諜並爆料說中國情報組織干預香港抗議和台灣選舉
," BBC News Chinese, 23 November 2019, accessed at: https://www.bbc.com/
zhongwen/trad/chinese-news-50528735

99 Reuters, Hong Kong's Press Freedom Ranking, accessed at: https://www.reuters
.com/graphics/HONGKONG-ANNIVERSARY/zdvxoejkxpx/index.html. Scores
for individual components of the ranking index of the latest two years can be
obtained from the website of Reporters Without Borders, accessed at: https://rsf
.org/en/country/hong-kong

100 Suzanne Pepper, The Dream of Genuine Universal Suffrage in Hong Kong Is
Gone for Good, but Can the Democracy Movement Survive?, *Hong Kong Free
Press*, 3 March 2021, accessed at: https://hongkongfp.com/2021/03/13/why-the
-dream-of-genuine-universal-suffrage-in-hong-kong-is-gone-for-good/

101 Hong Kong Public Opinion Research Institute, People's Trust in the Beijing
Central Government (12/1992–2/2023), accessed at: https://www.pori.hk/pop
-poll/trust-and-confidence-indicators-en/k002.html?lang=en

102 *Supra* note 52, 257.

103 Ibid, 258.

104 Hong Kong Monetary Authority, Hong Kong: The Global Offshore Renminbi
Business Hub, January 2016, accessed at: https://www.hkma.gov.hk/media/eng
/doc/key-functions/monetary-stability/rmb-business-in-hong-kong/hkma-rmb
-booklet.pdf

105 The idea of making "joint efforts by Guangdong, Hong Kong, and Macao to build
a quality living area in the Greater Pearl River Delta region" was first raised in
Chapter 54 of China's 13th Five-Year Plan, accessed at: http://en.ndrc.gov.cn/
newsrelease/201612/P020161207645765233498.pdf, before it was later officially
named as "Guangdong–Hong Kong–Macao Greater Bay Area." Ernst Young,
China, produced a briefing paper to help explain the official document, The Outline
Development Plan ("the Outline") for the Guangdong-Hong Kong-Macao Greater

Bay Area, available at: file:///C:/Users/user/Downloads/ey-guangdong-hong-kong -macau-greater-bay-area-from-connectivity-to-integration-en-20200323.pdf

106　See the website of World Bank's Development Data Group, *supra* note 71.

107　BBC News, "從《逃犯條例》到五大訴求：香港示威最新全景圖," 23 August 2019, accessed at: https://www.bbc.com/zhongwen/trad/chinese-news-49433303; Abby Seiff, Hong Kong's Fight for Independence, *International Bar Association*, 14 October 2019, accessed at: https://www.ibanet.org/article/A1E43459-235C -4F45-A54E-4019E516F13C

108　*Supra* note 8.

109　Ming-sho Ho, How Protests Evolve: Hong Kong's Anti-Extradition Movement and Lessons from the Umbrella Movement, *Mobilization: An International Journal*, 25(5), 711–728, 2020. Francis L. F. Lee, The Anti-Extradition Bill Protests and the Democracy Movement in Hong Kong, Asia Now, 19 July 2019, accessed at: https://www.asianstudies.org/the-anti-extradition-bill-protests-and -the-democracy-movement-in-hong-kong/

110　Reuters, Hong Kong Democrats Score a Landslide Local Election Landslide Victory after Months of Protests, 24 November 2019, accessed at: https://www .cnbc.com/2019/11/25/hong-kong-democrats-cheer-landslide-victory-in-local -elections.html; Emma Graham-Harrison, Hong Kong Voters Deliver Landslide Victory for Pro-Democracy Campaigners, *The Guardian*, 25 November 2019, accessed at: https://www.theguardian.com/world/2019/nov/24/hong-kong-resi-dents-turn-up-for-local-elections-in-record-numbers; Amy Gunia, Hong Kong's Democracy Parties Scored Big in Local Elections. Here's What That Means for Their Movement, *Time Magazine*, 25 November 2019, accessed at: https:// time.com/5736896/hong-kong-district-council-elections/; James Pomfret, Fresh Headache for China after Hong Kong Democrats Rout Pro-Beijing Candidates, Reuters, 25 November 2019, accessed at: https://www.reuters.com/article/us -hongkong-protests-election-analysis-idCAKBN1XZ0RB

111　Suzanne Pepper, Prof. Benny Tai's Next Masterplan? A Pro-Democrat Majority in Hong Kong's Legislature, *Hong Kong Free Press*, 25 April 2020, accessed at: https://hongkongfp.com/2020/04/25/prof-benny-tais-next-masterplan-a-pro -democrat-majority-in-hong-kongs-legislature/; Suzanne Pepper, Combating Factionalism and Annoying Beijing – Hong Kong's Benny Tai Has a Plan for Electoral Success, *Hong Kong Free Press*, 28 July 2020, accessed at: https:// hongkongfp.com/2020/07/28/combating-factionalism-and-annoying-beijing -hong-kongs-benny-tai-has-a-plan-for-electoral-success/; Ryan Tang, "Can Pan-Democrats Win a Majority in Hong Kong's September Elections?, *The China Project*, 22 July 2020, accessed at: https://thechinaproject.com/2020/07/22/hong -kongs-september-legislative-elections-explained/

112　Amnesty International, Hong Kong: Arbitrary Arrests, Brutal Beatings and Torture in Police Detention Revealed, 19 September 2019, accessed at: https:// www.amnesty.org/en/latest/press-release/2019/09/hong-kong-arbitrary-arrests -brutal-beatings-and-torture-in-police-detention-revealed/; Progressive Scholars Group, *Silencing Millions: Unchecked Violations of Internationally Recognized Human Rights by the Hong Kong Police Force*, 2020, accessed at: https://www .docdroid.net/0EA2Bhy/silencingmillions-text-final-pdf#page=46

113　陶嘉心, "反修例三周年 警方拘捕10278人 檢控率27% 1194人定罪," 香港01, 9 June 2022, accessed at: https://www.hk01.com/article/779307?utm_source =01articlecopy&utm_medium=referral

114　Reuters, Hong Kong Bans Public Gatherings of More Than Four People, 27 March 2020, accessed at: https://www.reuters.com/article/us-china-health-hong-kong-idUSKBN21E1MW. The SAR authorities were criticized as using social distancing regulations to prevent anti-government activities, see Iain Marlow and Jinshan Hong, Hong Kong Police Arrest Protesters for Violating Social Distancing Guidelines, *Time Magazine*, 11 May 2020, accessed at: https://time .com/5835103/hong-kong-protesters-coronavirus-restrictions/

115   BBC News, Hong Kong National Security Law: What Is It and Is It Worrying?, 28 June 2020, accessed at: https://www.bbc.com/news/world-asia-china-52765838; Amnesty International, Hong Kong's National Security Law: 10 Things You Need to Know, 17 July 2020, accessed at: https://www.amnesty.org/en/latest/ news/2020/07/hong-kong-national-security-law-10-things-you-need-to-know/

116   Candice Chau, 47 Democrats Charged with "Conspiracy to Commit Subversion" over Legislative Primaries, *Hong Kong Free Press*, 28 February 2021, accessed at: https://hongkongfp.com/2021/02/28/47-democrats-charged-with-conspiracy -to-commit-subversion-over-legislative-primaries/, and Human Rights Watch, Hong Kong: 47 Charged under Abusive Security Law, 2 March 2021, accessed at: https://www.hrw.org/news/2021/03/02/hong-kong-47-charged-under-abusive -security-law

117   Helen Davidson, Hong Kong Police Arrest Editor-in-Chief of Apple Daily Newspaper in Raids, *Guardian*, 17 June 2021, accessed at: https://www.theguard- ian.com/world/2021/jun/17/hong-kong-police-arrest-editor-in-chief-of-apple -daily-newspaper-in-morning-raids

118   Tom Grundy, Hong Kong Tiananmen Massacre Vigil Group Disbands Following Pressure from Authorities," *Hong Kong Free Press*, 26 September 2021, accessed at: https://hongkongfp.com/2021/09/25/breaking-hong-kong-tiananmen-massa- cre-vigil-group-disbands-following-pressure-from-authorities/

119   Reuters, Hong Kong Teachers' Union to Disband Due to "Drastic" Political Situation, 10 August 2021, accessed at: https://www.reuters.com/world/asia -pacific/hong-kong-teachers-union-disband-due-drastic-political-situation-2021 -08-10/; Amnesty International, Hong Kong: Closure of Prominent Rights Group Signals Worrying Domino Effect, 15 August 2021, accessed at: https://www .amnesty.org/en/latest/news/2021/08/hong-kong-disbandment-of-teachers-union -signals-spiralling-crackdown/

120   Reuters, Hong Kong Opposition Trade Union Group to Disband, 19 September 2021, accessed at: https://www.reuters.com/world/china/hong-kong-opposition -trade-union-group-disband-2021-09-19/ and Reuters, Hong Kong Trade Union Disbands as Impact of Security Law Deepens, 19 September 2021, accessed at: https://www.reuters.com/world/asia-pacific/hong-kong-trade-union-disbands -impact-security-law-deepens-2021-10-03/. For a brief analysis, see William Nee, The Crackdown on Trade Unions in Hong Kong: What Response from Responsible Investors?, Cambridge Core Blog, 19 April 2022, accessed at: https:// www.cambridge.org/core/blog/2022/04/19/the-crackdown-on-trade-unions-in -hong-kong-what-response-from-responsible-investors/

121   Timeline: 58 Hong Kong Civil Society Groups Disband Following the Onset of the Security Law, *Hong Kong Free Press*, 30 June 2021, accessed at: https:// hongkongfp.com/2022/06/30/explainer-over-50-groups-gone-in-11-months -how-hong-kongs-pro-democracy-forces-crumbled/;   Congressional-Executive Commission on China, Hong Kong's Civil Society: From an Open City to a City of Fear, Special Report, October 2022, accessed at:https://www.cecc.gov/publica- tions/commission-analysis/hong-kong%E2%80%99s-civil-society-from-an-open -city-to-a-city-of-fear; Patrick Poon, The Crushing of Hong Kong's Civil Society Will Be Felt By All, *Nikkei Asia*, 24 July 2022, accessed at: https://asia.nikkei .com/Opinion/The-crushing-of-Hong-Kong-s-civil-society-will-be-felt-by-all

122   United Nations Human Rights Committee (135th sess.: 2022: Geneva), Concluding Observations on the 4th Periodic Report of Hong Kong, China:

Human Rights Committee, 11 November 2022 accessed at: https://digitallibrary
.un.org/record/4002782

123 BBC News, Hong Kong: Activist with Cancer Jailed for Olympic Protest Attempt,
12 July 2022, accessed at: https://www.bbc.com/news/world-asia-62132267

124 Selina Cheng, Covid-19: Hong Kong National Security Police Arrest 2 for
Sedition over Anti-Vaxx Posts, *Hong Kong Free Press*, 25 February 2022,
accessed at: https://hongkongfp.com/2022/02/25/covid-19-hong-kong-national
-security-police-arrest-2-for-sedition-over-anti-vaxx-posts/

125 *The Japan Times*, Hong Kong Sees Surge in Charges under Colonial Sedition
Law, 24 August 2022, accessed at: https://www.japantimes.co.jp/news/2022/08
/24/asia-pacific/hong-kong-supercharges-sedition-law/. In a more serious case,
the convicted was sent to jail for nine years, see BBC News, "Liberate Hong
Kong": The Slogan That Will Land You in Jail, 31 July 2021, accessed at: https://
www.bbc.com/news/world-asia-china-58009605

126 Kelly Ho, 5 Hong Kong Speech Therapists Found Guilty of Sedition over
Children's Books, *Hong Kong Free Press*, 7 September 2022, accessed at: https://
hongkongfp.com/2022/09/07/breaking-5-hong-kong-speech-therapists-found
-guilty-of-sedition-over-childrens-books/; Sum Lok-kei, Hong Kong Therapists
Convicted of Sedition over Children's Books, *The Guardian*, 7 September
2022, accessed at: https://www.theguardian.com/world/2022/sep/07/hong-kong
-authors-of-childrens-books-sheep-wolves-convicted-of-sedition

127 A special page containing related news articles on the trial of *Stand News* can
be found in Hong Kong's Stand News Trial, *Hong Kong Free Press*, accessed
at: https://hongkongfp.com/hong-kongs-stand-news-trial/. A brief history of
Stand News is available at Timeline: Hong Kong's Non-Profit Outlet Stand News
through the Years, *Hong Kong Free Press*, 5 January 2022, accessed at:https://
hongkongfp.com/2022/01/05/timeline-hong-kongs-non-profit-outlet-stand-news
-through-the-years/

128 inmediahk.net, "國安法三年. 數據分析," 3 July 2023, accessed at: https://
www.inmediahk.net/node/%E7%A4%BE%E9%81%8B/%E3%80%90%E5%9C
%8B%E5%AE%89%E6%B3%95%E4%B8%89%E5%B9%B4%EF%BC%8E
%E6%95%B8%E6%93%9A%E5%88%86%E6%9E%90%E3%80%91259%E4
%BA%BA%E8%A2%AB%E6%8D%95-71%E4%BA%BA%E6%B6%89%E7
%85%BD%E5%8B%95-%E5%AE%9A%E7%BD%AA%E7%8E%87%E7%99
%BE%E5%88%86%E7%99%BE

129 Hong Kong's Publishers Self-Censor in Wake of National Security Law, *Financial
Times*, 19 July 2020 accessed at: https://www.ft.com/content/f1352a8a-3931
-4160-99f2-af7bbe5b67db; Angeli Datt, The Impact of the National Security
Law on Media and Internet Freedom in Hong Kong, 8 September 2021, accessed
at: https://freedomhouse.org/article/impact-national-security-law-media-and
-internet-freedom-hong-kong; Rhoda Kwan, "It's about Self-Censorship": Hong
Kong Counsellors Struggle to Navigate Security Law Concerns, *Hong Kong Free
Press*, 24 December 2021, accessed at: https://hongkongfp.com/2021/08/22/hong
-kong-counsellors-struggle-to-navigate-security-law-concerns/; Mona Wang and
Jonathan Mayer, Self-Censorship Under Law: A Case Study of the Hong Kong
National Security Law, *Free and Open Communication on the Internet* 2023(1).
46-55, 2023, accessed at: https://doi.org/10.48550/arXiv.2210.11636

130 Hong Kong: Crackdown on Vigils to Commemorate 1989 Tiananmen Square
Massacre Show Beijing's Fear of the Power of Memory, *The Conversation*, 5
June 2023, accessed at: https://theconversation.com/hong-kong-crackdown-on
-vigils-to-commemorate-1989-tiananmen-square-massacre-show-beijings-fear
-of-the-power-of-memory-207037

131 Verna Yu, Hong Kong Political Cartoonist Axed after 40 Years Following Criticism from Officials, *The Guardian*, 12 May 2023, accessed at: https://www.theguardian.com/world/2023/may/12/hong-kong-political-cartoonist-axed-after-40-years-following-criticism-from-officials

132 "I Will Continue until I Have No Other Choice": The Art of Bookselling under Hong Kong's National Security Law, *Hong Kong Free Press*, 25 July 2020, accessed at: https://hongkongfp.com/2020/07/25/i-will-continue-until-i-have-no-other-choice-the-art-of-bookselling-under-hong-kongs-national-security-law/; Self-Censorship Hits Hong Kong Book Fair in Wake of National Security Law, *The Guardian*, 25 July 2021, accessed at: https://www.theguardian.com/books/2021/jul/15/self-censorship-hits-hong-kong-book-fair-in-wake-of-national-security-law

133 Wenyi Zhang, Number of Selected Books Which Written By Democracy Activists Removed from Public Libraries after the National Security Law Imposed in Hong Kong as of July 4, 2020, *Statista*, July 2020 accessed at: https://www.statista.com/statistics/1130934/hong-kong-impact-of-national-security-law-on-democracy-activist-books-in-public-libraries/; "Not Recommended" Reading: The Books Hong Kong Is Purging from Public Libraries, *Hong Kong Free Press*, 3 June 2023, accessed at: https://hongkongfp.com/2023/05/26/not-recommended-reading-the-books-hong-kong-is-purging-from-public-libraries/; Removal of Political Books Sparks Alarm in Hong Kong, *La Prensa Latina Media*, 23 May 2023, accessed at: https://www.laprensalatina.com/removal-of-political-books-sparks-alarm-in-hong-kong/

134 Hong Kong Teachers Told to Inform on Students, Colleagues in Free Speech Crackdown, *Radio Free Asia*, 21 December 2021, accessed at: https://www.rfa.org/english/news/china/teachers-12212022151837.html

135 Reuters, Hong Kong to Censor Films under National Security Law, 11 June 2021, accessed at: https://www.reuters.com/world/asia-pacific/hong-kong-censor-films-under-national-security-law-2021-06-11/; Screening of Taiwanese Documentary Axed at Hong Kong Film Festival after Censors Request Removal of Protest Scenes, *Hong Kong Free Press*, 25 October 2022, accessed at: https://hongkongfp.com/2022/10/25/screening-of-taiwanese-documentary-axed-at-hong-kong-film-festival-after-censors-request-removal-of-protest-scenes/; Rebecca Davis and Patrick Frater, Hong Kong Passes Film Law Allowing Censorship on National Security Grounds, *Variety*, 27 October 2021, accessed at: https://variety.com/2021/film/asia/hong-kong-censorship-ban-national-security-films-1235099155/

136 Hong Kong Labour Day Protest Called off after Organizer's Brief Disappearance, Global Voices, 27 April 2023, accessed at: https://globalvoices.org/2023/04/27/hong-kong-labour-day-protest-called-off-after-organizers-brief-disappearance/; Christopher Siu-tat Mung, May 1 Labor Day Demonstration Still a No-Go in Hong Kong, *The Diplomat*, 29 April 2023, accessed at: https://thediplomat.com/2023/04/may-1-labor-day-demonstration-still-a-no-go-in-hong-kong/

137 Human Rights Watch, Dismantling a Free Society: Hong Kong One Year after the National Security Law, 2020, accessed at: https://www.hrw.org/feature/2021/06/25/dismantling-free-society/hong-kong-one-year-after-national-security-law

3 Media, Internet, and the Civil Movement in Hong Kong

Control and protest (part 1: control)

In Chapter 2, we explored the historical background of Hong Kong people's high hopes for progressive democracy, even after the takeover by an authoritarian regime with no track record of democracy or freedom of speech. They relied on the commitment signed by both the coloniser British government and the Chinese regime. Though Hong Kong people were not consulted or represented in the Sino-British talks over Hong Kong's future, and despite all the controversies in the pre-handover years, the ruling Chinese Communist Party (CCP) did indeed sign an internationally recognised diplomatic document – the Sino-British Joint Declaration (JD) – with Britain concerning Hong Kong's future after 1997. But once in charge, China started to erode all the pledges, including "one country, two systems" (OCTS) – "Hong Kong people ruling Hong Kong," freedom of speech, freedom of assembly and market economy and independent judiciary for at least 50 years after the handover. For instance, in the year 2003, just five years after rejoining the motherland, the first Chief Executive, Tung Chee-hwa tried to ram through national security legislation required by Article 23 of the Hong Kong Basic Law. More than half a million Hong Kong citizens took to the streets to protest; the National Security bill was then indefinitely postponed.[1] In 2017, the Chinese foreign minister rejected the JD document as void.[2] And in 2023, Xia Baolong, the director of the Hong Kong and Macau Affairs Office, said Hong Kong should not focus on small advantages but look at the bigger interest of the country. In other words, one country, two systems was reinterpreted: upholding the one country took priority over the two systems.[3]

After more than a quarter-century of rule by China, Hong Kong people, in particular the younger generation, finally awakened and took their fate into their own hands. They summoned the strength to form a social movement across all walks of life, in which they insisted "if we don't win, we would rather die." They also said "better be ashes than dust."[4] The determination to sacrifice for the cause of democracy was unprecedented. A popular slogan advocated by radical or confrontational protesters was "if we burn, you burn with us," which actually meant "mutual destruction."[5] Previously, the compromising pan-democrats and radical activists were divided in their strategy

DOI: 10.4324/9781003150244-3

towards the authorities. The gap narrowed in the 2019 social movement as the conflict with the government became increasingly acute. They openly called for reconciliation and claimed "peaceful [camp] and military/valiant [camp] will not split" in the face of a violent and heavy crackdown by the authorities on everyone, without differentiation. And nobody broke ranks to negotiate or compromise with the oppressor.[6]

Apple Daily played a crucial role in securing this cohesion. The pro-democratic newspaper put the young protesters in a better light as fighters for democracy with violent means, saying that they loved Hong Kong and were willing to sacrifice their own lives.[7] Proprietor Jimmy Lai was "very supportive of young people." There was an advertisement in the newspaper titled "Support students to subscribe to *Apple Daily*."[8] According to witness Cheung Kim-hung in Lai's high-profile national security and sedition trial, the campaign aimed to encourage readers to subsidise young people's subscriptions to *Apple Daily*.[9] Lai also set an editorial policy that promoted "cohesion" between peaceful and valiant protesters during the 2019 protests, Cheung said. The prosecution witness previously said that Lai had full control over editorial decision-making at *Apple Daily*. We shall elaborate the role of *Apple Daily* and its proprietor, Jimmy Lai, more later.

Burnt generation and mutual destruction

We would like to name these young activists a "burnt generation" (a comparison to the "beat generation" cited in Kerouac's *On the Road*) who were prepared to sacrifice their youth and future for their cause. This will be further explained in the next chapter.[10]

Gwyneth Ho was a non-violent activist who was prosecuted for taking a lit candle to Victoria Park on June 4 2020, after the traditional commemoration of the victims of the Tiananmen Massacre had been banned.[11] According to her explanation in court of the term "mutual destruction" it meant "we are prepared to sacrifice" so mainland China will react or overreact with an even more austere and extreme policy in Hong Kong. Then people in the world and in Hong Kong would see the CCP's real face and not derive false hope from its promises.[12] According to this line of thinking, the CCP would destroy Hong Kong's social infrastructure further and this would lead to stronger sanctions from foreign countries on Hong Kong ministers, judges and senior officers.[13]

Activists supported a Bill of Sanctions proposed by bipartisan Senators and Congressmen in the US on key figures in Hong Kong, including officials, senior judges, judges selected for national security cases, and prosecutors in national security and sedition cases.[14] Some international media endorsed this idea; for instance *The Economist*, which said that China no longer treasured Hong Kong as a financial hub.[15]

To replace the century old Common Law with mainland Chinese National Security Law

China is crushing Hong Kong's most important pillar of civil society, which is the rule of law. To replace it, they approved the National Security Law (NSL) to be implemented in Hong Kong, which in effect violated many of Hong Kong's Common Law traditions, including the presumption of innocence, the right to jury trial, the right to bail, and the right to a court hearing within 48 hours of being taken into custody. In terms of national security law Hong Kong is now just another Chinese city.[16] This view of not treasuring Hong Kong's unique position, by coincidence, was also shared by a veteran mainland Chinese economist Xu Cheng-gang, who adopted a critical analysis of China's current economic policies, with a passing reference to Hong Kong. He said Chinese authorities no longer treasured Hong Kong once it posed a threat to the ruling regime.[17] To recap his analysis very briefly, he said that in the view of the CCP, economic development started in the early 1980s would eventually lead to a "peaceful revolution": a "capitalistic" way of doing things which would pose a threat to the CCP. For this reason, the CCP feared the development of private ownership and sought to restrict it. The CCP actually stopped the expansion of private business around 2006 and 2007 and favoured state-owned enterprises over private ones, and this had been effective. If a private enterprise grew too big, the CCP would control and restrict it, as with Alibaba. No exception could be made for Hong Kong.[18]

Another young Hong Kong politician, Winnie Yu, was also asked in court what she understood by "mutual destruction" She said it was to force the HKSAR government to come to the negotiation table and let "Hong Kong [interest] be the first."[19] This idea was of course rejected by party media such as *Global Times*.[20] In the wake of the social movement in 2019, the Central government and the Hong Kong SAR government escalated the pressure and used repressive measures to destroy Hong Kong's social infrastructure and dismantle the city's liberal way of living built over a century and a half upon the rule of law, freedom of speech and free media. In short, there is no more freedom of the [critical/oppositional] press as we can see in the persecution of Jimmy Lai, the outspoken tycoon of popular *Apple Daily*. As compared with mainland China, Hong Kong still maintains a very limited freedom of speech. There is no more freedom of assembly because no unionist or activist dares to organise one. Worse still, the independence of the judiciary is doubtful after the imposition of the NSL in June 2020 and electoral changes designed to produce a compliant and patriotic legislature. There is neither any check or balance of the three powers – administrative, legislative, and judicial – nor an effective fourth estate holding the administration accountable.

Hong Kong's Fourth Estate deteriorating and 60 civil institutes shut down

Regarding the fourth estate, media, it is either under tremendous pressure to "shut down" or to buy survival by abstaining from independent critical and truth-seeking news reports. According to Reporters Sans Frontières (RSF), Hong Kong's press freedom ranking has fallen to 140 out of 180 countries, a dramatic low level.[21] Furthermore, many long-standing civil society organisations have either been shut down or forced to close. The casualties total 60, including three traditional pillars of civil society, the Professional Teachers Union (PTU), Confederation of Workers Unions, and Hong Kong Alliance to Support Democracy in China, as well as pro-democracy political parties such as the Civic Party[22] and NGOs including Amnesty International Hong Kong.[23] The PTU managed to save its property assets and bank savings by closing voluntarily. A year after the closure, the Union distributed HK$3,190 to each remaining registered member.[24] NGOs as a source of information for the media are much diminished. Survivors are reluctant to be whistleblowers or dare not criticise the authorities. As for foreign countries, Chinese leaders and indeed the Hong Kong government have repeatedly warned against colluding with foreign agents. This has been a common accusation of those who dared to air critical views.[25] In connection with media, internet, and the social movement, in this chapter we shall examine the demise of the two leading pro-democracy media, namely the popular tabloid *Apple Daily* and the leading pro-democracy digital news site *Stand News*.

Our attempt here is not so much about the politics itself. Our concern is more about how media and social media played a part in this unprecedented civil movement, and the prosecution they suffered from speaking up. As the authorities fuelled the social movement with more repression, the movement rapidly spread to even more people. The escalation then attracted more repressive measures. Suspicions were reported that some of these had been out-sourced, to vigilante groups such as the white-clad men who attacked commuters and protesters on 21 July 2019. This vicious circle produced a rapid escalation of controlling strategies and tactics to suppress the movement. The most powerful weapon, of course, was the imposition of the NSL in Hong Kong by China, with neither consultation nor the normal procedure of going through the purged "all-patriots" Legislative Council.[26]

Introduction

In late July 2023, Jimmy Lai, the 75-year-old jailed proprietor of the defunct pro-democracy newspaper *Apple Daily* was seen half-naked walking inside the high-security Stanley prison. That was part of his precious 50 minutes in the open space of the prison, according to an *Associated Press* caption. For the remaining 23 hours, he would be confined alone in a cell, without even a fan in summer heat of 35 degrees Celsius or more. He had been in captivity for more than a thousand days. He was allowed visits from relatives twice a month for up to 30 minutes.[27] His alleged crime was fraud, for which he was convicted and sentenced to more than five years behind bars. Still to come were several charges under the NSL related to sedition and collusion with foreign forces. This trial was postponed twice from Sept 2022 to December 2023 while lawyers argued over whether he could be represented by a King's Counsel from the UK. This was eventually refused.[28]

Jimmy Lai's trial in Hong Kong

The Associated Press photo of Lai in prison was published on 14 August 2023, when Lai and a handful of prominent Hong Kong political figures appeared in court on charges of "organising and leading an illegal assembly" back on 18 August 2019[29] when the social movement was at its peak. An estimated 1.7 million citizens took to the streets to air their grievances towards the Hong Kong and Central governments regarding a later withdrawn extradition bill, which would have allowed the Hong Kong government to extradite fugitive suspects to China for trial. Lai's prison regime became harsher after his latest situation was exposed by the AP photo.[30] Jimmy Lai is a self-made entrepreneur-turned-media tycoon. His involvement in politics and critical views of China could be traced back to the 1989 Tiananmen massacre, during which he wrote some highly critical articles in his newly founded *Next Magazine*. He was born in a well-off family in Guangdong province. But his parents were ill-fated; his father was persecuted and the family became poor due to political struggles in China. Lai came to Hong Kong as a 12-year-old and became rich through hard work and talent. He never forgot that his opportunities were actually provided by a liberal colonial Hong Kong. According to numerous English news reports, and the last documentary filmed before he was jailed, he said he owed his success in life to the freedom in Hong Kong.

During the political transition before the handover in 1997, traditional media either shifted position or withdrew from the market altogether. So his *Apple Daily* was regarded by many critics as the only pro-democracy newspaper after the handover.[31] The previously pluralistic media market, ranging across the political spectrum from pro-Taiwan to independent to pro-Beijing, had contracted to pro-establishment or pro-Beijing. Previously critical or daring news media prepared to criticise mainland China had subsided or been axed.[32] Lai saw a market gap which he could fill. According to his former publisher and senior aid Yip Yat-kin, "Hong Kong people very much wish to have universal suffrage. Democracy has a market so Jimmy sells it."[33]

Having acquired his wealth, Lai was looking for a new direction and meaning of life. He started in media when he launched his weekly *Next Magazine*. His bold and risk-taking way of doing business brought immediate success.

Tabloid scandalous reports mixed with investigative news reports and critical political opinion earned popularity and he created a new brand of media willing to hold the governments of Hong Kong and China, accountable.[34] After the success of *Next*, Lai founded his flagship – the controversial tabloid *Apple Daily* – in 1995. It quickly won a big slice of the market and some small and minor papers struggled to survive as a result. Many shut down.[35] On the one hand, he uncovered scandalous news by employing teams of paparazzi, which attracted criticism. On the other, having a political view was less controversial; most papers had a political stance.

In the late 1990s and early millennium, the market for newspapers providing only entertainment and information disappeared. All seemed to have to adopt a political position or take sides in order to survive. Part of the reason was that Hong Kong had become highly politicised.[36] Lai was a rich man who had already enjoyed success and fame. But he was prepared to take up the democracy cause. In 2003, he was heavily involved in mobilising people to object to the national security bill which, after half a million people took to the streets, was postponed indefinitely. *Apple Daily* designed and delivered free posters for protesters to carry. Lai himself was often seen carrying a banner alongside his pan-democrat friends and aides.

In September 2014 when the Occupy Central or Umbrella Movement began, he went to the occupy district of Admiralty/Central and was seen there almost every day. He often walked at the head of protests with Democratic Party founder Martin Lee Chu-ming and Cardinal Joseph Zen. According to the pro-CCP camp and media, he was the mastermind of the "gang of four" in Hong Kong.[37] He also regularly attended the annual candle-lit vigil to remember the victims of the 1989 Tiananmen massacre. Before the promulgation of the NSL in 2020, Hong Kong was the only territory on Chinese soil where thousands of people could gather to commemorate the incident.[38]

In the summer of 2019 things took a drastic turn. Lai put his own personal security at stake by getting further into politics. This time he went to the West to lobby for Hong Kong democracy.[39] Besides using his daily newspaper to back the protesters, and in particular the pan-democrats, he took up the task of international lobbying. He visited the US and urged senior politicians to sanction Hong Kong officials.[40]

Something haunting in the air: Rumours spread that *Apple Daily* had to shut down before July 1 2020

Because of his pursuit of Hong Kong democracy, Lai became known as a fighter for democracy as well as a media tycoon. As a result, he was targeted by the pro-Beijing media. More importantly, he was regarded as the "mastermind," "ringleader," or "troublemaker" and was often the target of threats to him, his family, and his staff. He was injured by one attacker and protesters besieged his house. He and his visitors were constantly watched.[41] There were constant rumours after the handover that he would be arrested and punished, but he refused to leave Hong Kong. In his own words, he was a "trouble-maker." He could not possibly make trouble and leave Hong Kong. He would stay and fight for Hong Kong's freedom and democracy. To a certain extent, he still trusted the judicial system in Hong Kong, that the rule of law established by the British colonisers would give him a fair trial.[42]

When Jimmy Lai turned 76 in December 2023, his son Sebastian, lobbying in the US and UK, feared his ill health might lead to his death in jail.[43] Things did change drastically one year after the 2019 social movement. In 2020 a new national security law was passed in Beijing without any local consultation, even of the pro-Beijing camp. Since the law was passed more than 260 people have been jailed in the name of national security.[44] Hong Kong can be said to have the most "political prisoners" of all Chinese cities. The government has put more than a thousand people behind bars since 2019.[45] Never before in Hong Kong have so many ordinary men and women, young and old, middle-aged, professionals or amateurs, middle class or grassroots been jailed because of their expression, participation in a social movement, or to put it simply, fighting for a better future for Hong Kong.

Hong Kong disturbances and riots since the 1960s

The 2019 protests were the biggest popular uprising since the late 1960s, when the leftist or pro-Beijing people took to the streets to protest against British colonial rule. During that time, many were arrested and sentenced to prison. But most of them were released within two years. The British Hong Kong government also used emergency powers to make exceptional rules, but those prisoners were either deported or released after lobbying from London and Beijing.[46] After that, the British Hong Kong administration adopted a series of "soft landing administrative policies" to restore public order and win back public trust. It built affordable housing, began to set up district-level elections, and introduced directly and indirectly elected seats in municipal, district, and legislative level elections, to allow more public participation in the decision-making process.[47] Unlike its predecessor, the HKSAR government disregarded the public's five demands, and turned a deaf ear to local and foreign lobbying for the release of Jimmy Lai.[48]

Lai has been in jail for 1,000 days; the UK, US and other foreign countries have urged the Hong Kong government to release him. One foreign media editorial said the publisher's bravery had exposed China's false promises to Hong Kong.[49] Hong Kong citizens may not easily forget the alarming image of 200 police officers arriving in the *Apple Daily* news building to confiscate all the computers in the newsroom and boxes of editorial files. Lai was escorted back to the office chained round the waist and handcuffed, while *Apple Daily* journalists recorded this unprecedented raid by the authorities. His wife, Teresa Li, messaged a close family friend, saying it was a heart-breaking spectacle;

they wanted to humiliate him. But the friend replied that Hong Kong people would see that as a badge of honour.[50]

In November 2023, Jimmy Lai was awarded the Magnitsky Human Rights award.[51] At about the same time, Tonyee Chow Hang-tung received a Human Rights Award from the Council of Bars and Law Societies of Europe (CCBE).[52] The awards were to honour "the long-standing and outstanding commitment and sacrifice these lawyers have demonstrated in upholding the fundamental values of the legal profession and in defending and advocating for human rights and the respect for the rule of law," it said.[53]

Chow, who organized now-banned annual vigils commemorating the 1989 Tiananmen massacre, said in an acceptance speech sent from prison that the fight for democracy in China was part of ensuring that the law serves democratic and humanitarian values, rather than just the wishes of those willing to use force. She is currently awaiting trial under the NSL on charges of subversion. Rights activists said that the fact that Chow was honoured alongside two mainland lawyers showed how little difference there is now between the judicial systems in Hong Kong and mainland China, following the crackdown on political opposition and dissent since the 2019 protest movement. In December 2023, Chow was placed in solitary confinement for 18 days, allegedly for receiving too many letters in the festive season.[54] In the second half of 2023, she suffered similar punishment almost every month, which meant no social activities in prison like spending an hour in the fresh air, no newspapers or books, and no TV or radio. She would receive only meals.[55] Her friends said on her Facebook page that they thought the frequent punishments were due to her receiving two prominent human rights awards, plus her relentless presence on social media via supporters and friends, and her bid to participate as a related party in the injunction case of "Glory to Hong Kong."[56] In other words, international lobbying and speaking up did put pressure on the HKSAR government.

Besides Jimmy Lai, his six most senior editorial staff were also detained. All seven defendants have since been in custody for more than two years without trial and without bail, because the NSL allows a judge to detain defendants on the basis that they may harm national security if free. This is contradictory to the Common Law in which the suspect is supposed to be innocent until proven otherwise, and it is up to the prosecutor to show why bail should be denied.

The NSL has changed Hong Kong's independent judiciary because in national security cases all the judges are selected by the administration. Under new legal aid rules, defendants cannot choose their own counsel. Nor can Jimmy Lai, who has appealed twice to have a King's Counsel from London to defend for him, without success. The Bar Association and prominent lawyers argued that this would not offend national security since there are overseas judges sitting on the court of appeal and higher courts, not to mention that there are numerous barristers and solicitors from overseas who practice in

Hong Kong.[57] Though not as many as before, perhaps. After pressure on legal practitioners accused of supporting or defending protesters, some foreign lawyers and legal firms have moved away from Hong Kong.[58]

Another case concerned a photographer who had lived in Hong Kong for more than three decades. He was arrested, charged, and acquitted but he was refused his legal expenses usually awarded to acquitted defendants as a matter of course – even though he won his case. The government has appealed to higher courts and the case has continued for four years. As of November 2023, he was still fighting for half a million dollars from the authorities.[59] Before we move on to talk about the strategies and tactics the authorities used to control and suppress media, we shall consider a major online media outlet, *Stand News,* which was forced to shut down because of the arrest of the two chief editors and freezing of its bank account.

Stand News: The alleged plan B of *Apple Daily* by Beijing-funded media

Chung Pui-kuen, was the founding chief editor of *Stand News.* Chung and his colleague, Patrick Lam, acting chief editor of *Stand News*, were both detained for 11 and ten months respectively before their sedition trial in 2023.[60] In late November, the judge of the *Stand News* case should have delivered his verdict, but this was further postponed to 2024 to await the verdict of another sedition case appeal. The judge said he did not want to give an "inappropriate" sentence when there was an upcoming verdict from a higher court. If he gave a verdict, he had to give a sentence. He concluded that it would be better to wait for the appeal court verdict concerning an internet personality's non-violent inciting sedition case.[61]

The pro-Beijing media repeatedly linked *Apple Daily* and *Stand News,* alleging that the former had funded the latter, as the so-called plan B of *Apple Daily.* When this was put to the former chief editor, Chung Pui-kuen, he said it was a smear.[62] But both the *Apple Daily* and *Stand News* were regarded as pro-democracy media, which in the eyes of pro-Beijing politicians or prosecutors were serving "foreign forces" and using Hong Kong as a "base of subversion" to "act against China and disturb Hong Kong" – as prosecutor Ng Shuk-kuen said in the *Stand News* court case.[63] The alleged crime of Chung Pui-Kuen was apparently conspiring with Patrick Lam to print 17 seditious articles to incite hatred of the Hong Kong SAR government and the Central government, though seditious intent was not proven in court. The verdict was due to be pronounced in early October but was since postponed to mid-November, then further to April 2024 and beyond.[64]

So why were these two media targeted by the police and the authorities? First of all, according to many Hong Kong journalists, the police "hated" Hong Kong media, in particular *Apple Daily* and *Stand News,* during the 2019 social movement, when the former had a team of 100 on breaking news while the latter news outlet had crews doing live streaming.[65] This produced "unfiltered and unedited live videos" showing police brutality and violence towards the protesters with an abundance of weapons, and the escalation of repressive measures. Critical coverage continued in the ensuing three years, as the police started to purge democratic politicians by using the NSL and putting up million-dollar rewards for the arrest of exiles[66].

Crime: News reporting?

The raids and arrests targeting *Apple Daily* gave the outside world an impression that the leading popular newspaper had committed a serious crime: to report the truth about the 2019 social movement. And Hong Kong press freedom was dying or endangered. Half a year later in Dec. 2021, when another 200-strong police squad descended on the office of *Stand News*, international media found the blow to Hong Kong media unrepairable. Two chief editors and a news editor were taken away for interrogation while the two chief editors were arrested.[67] Altogether 600 journalists lost their jobs during the closure of *Apple Daily*. When *Stand News* died, several dozen more journalists joined them. Media workers who took a very grim look at the media industry thought that they might also be arrested and chose to leave their homes, family members, and belongings behind. They fled immediately to foreign countries. The chilling effect caused some people to shut down their social media accounts or pull down any images they took in 2019, or before. Under the JD and the Basic Law mini-constitution, Hong Kong media were allowed to exercise the freedom of the press. However, the traditional media was losing the younger generation, who were fed up with the lack of progress in democratic development. The "compromising and criticising" approach by the pan-democrats was regarded as a weak approach by the younger generation because they had made little progress in getting universal suffrage or democracy for Hong Kong.[68]

However, *Stand News*, as a relatively small but innovative digital media outlet, aired many bloggers' points of view. Also, live streaming was followed by many watchers, which boosted their viewer and circulation figures tremendously. With surging subscriptions, especially in 2019, *Stand News* could actually double their reporting team and rented a larger office.[69]

One of the most popular reporters in *Stand News* was Gwyneth Ho, otherwise known as "Sister of *Stand News*." Thanks to Ho's live streaming people could see the disproportionate violence employed by the police and assess the injustice with their own eyes. On 21 July 2019, Ho became famous when she live streamed the mass assault by thugs in white tee-shirts on ordinary citizens in an underground station in Yuen Long in the New Territories of Hong Kong. She carried on even when she was being beaten by the white-clad gang and had blood dripping from her head. During a court hearing on her role as a reporter-turned-activist, Gwyneth Ho said she was not a heroine. She was only a medium who carried the news of the courage of hundreds and thousands of protesters confronting the police and the white-clad gangs beating up several dozen commuters including herself, by live streaming the assault.[70] She said she became famous because of the bravery of ordinary citizens; she was not the heroine. She was just a reporter. When she decided to participate in politics, she thought she needed to resign from her job as a reporter. She wanted to be genuine and complete in her choice of role.[71]

On 1 July 2019, hundreds and thousands of protesters gathered outside the Hong Kong Legislative Council building, while some radical protesters attempted to use force to break into the entrance. Then legislators including Claudia Mo, a former journalist turned legislator, tried to convince and block these young people from using force to get access to the legislature.[72] After nine hours or more, the protesters managed to get access to the chamber. Surprisingly no police kept them out or turned up to expel them. After midnight, some protesters held a vote and decided to leave the chamber after some destruction of furniture, paintings, and accessories. A handful of protesters decided to stay behind. This was a delicate moment when some protesters decided to go back and forcibly carry out those who refused to leave. During this very unusual moment, Gwyneth Ho continued to live-feed even though she herself broke into tears at this extremely dangerous and precious moment of some people risking their own lives to help save others.[73]

The assault on ordinary commuters on July 21 was alarming partly due to the fact that no police appeared for as long as 39 minutes, even after hundreds of citizens had telephoned the police emergency line and some had even visited the police station in person. The few policemen who passed by were seen walking away from the crime. After the live streaming and serious injuries were widely circulated, the Hong Kong public realised that the pursuit of public order did not include protection for them, in the once safe city of Hong Kong. Citizens were both shocked and disappointed that the authorities also refused to set up an independent inquiry into this matter. Some decided at that moment they had to take care of themselves, and leave the city with their family for good.[74]

Gwyneth Ho was actually attacked by one of the white-clad guys with a stick. Her head injury needed a dozen stitches. She refused to leave the scene and continued to report live until the then chief editor of *Stand News*, Chung Pui-kuen, arrived an hour later.[75] Chung took her to the emergency ward of a nearby hospital. He said she was lucky that a photographer was protecting her during the attack. Otherwise she would have suffered a more serious head injury.[76] Two years after the terrifying assault on ordinary citizens, the official account of the Yuen Long mob had shifted narratives from "violent attack" to "gang fight."[77]

"Brother of *Stand News*"

Ronson Chan, chairperson of Hong Kong Journalists Association (HKJA) and deputy news editor of *Stand News,* was arrested for interrogation when his two heads, former chief editor Chung Pui-kuen and incumbent chief editor, Patrick Lam were arrested on 29 December 2021[78] In a BBC documentary on Hong Kong press freedom, Chan featured as a daring on the spot journalist who, on several occasions when covering confrontations between police and protesters, was targeted by police tear gas. He would shout back and argue with the police media team when Hong Kong journalists were ill-treated by rank and file police.[79] Like Gwyneth Ho, Ronson Chan specialised in live streaming. He once complained on his Facebook page that Ho was an "independent mind" and did not follow agreed arrangements. Sometimes when they had agreed in advance where they should go he would see her in another place where she shouldn't be. But both of them were passionate journalists who would devote themselves night and day to covering the movement. In a radio live broadcast when asked about the allegedly HK$60million accumulated in *Stand News's* bank account, Chan was so overwhelmed with emotion that he sobbed, explaining that the money actually came from audience support. Over several months he and many of his colleagues were on the street covering the latest developments, from early morning till very late at night. The audience appreciated their work and supported *Stand News's* revenue.[80]

Targetting *Apple Daily* and *Stand News*: The two leading pro-democracy media

In early 2021, there was a rumour that *Apple Daily* would be shut down before 1 July 2021, the anniversary of Hong Kong's return to China in 1997. Many *Apple Daily* journalists were anxious. But the senior management assured them that *Apple Daily* would continue to report and print as long as the Hong Kong audience continued to support them. *Apple Daily* even rejected some in-house journalists' suggestion that as a precaution against sudden closure of the paper they should be made redundant so they could get their severance pay. And they could remain in the job as contracted staff. Some staff left because the employer refused this special arrangement. A major reason why *Apple Daily* could not possibly make their staff redundant and re-employ them again was because *Apple Daily* was a listed company in the Hong Kong Stock Exchange and was restricted by listing company rules. Also management still trusted the Hong Kong government and the rule of law in Hong Kong.[81] Two or three years later, journalists are still talking about this episode. We shall analyse the approach adopted by the authorities when we talk about the control tactics and strategies later in this chapter.

The enormous power of media, internet, and social media helped to spread the "being water" social movement in 2019. Exactly three decades before, Hong Kong people had seen the crackdown on the Beijing student movement. In 1989, a million Hong Kong people took to the streets to demonstrate their support for the Beijing students. They shouted "1989 Beijing was the future of Hong Kong."[82] In 2019, commentators usually identified the demonstrations as the largest turn-out protest in Hong Kong since the Tiananmen Square massacre protests in 1989. The scope, scale, and frequency were also unprecedented.[83] In 2019, from June until November and December, protests happened on a weekly and later daily basis. After the most fierce confrontations on the campuses of the Chinese University of Hong Kong and Hong Kong Polytechnic University in November which involved hundreds and thousands of students, the movement died down for a while.[84]

Then came COVID-19 with regulations restricting gatherings and requiring masks. Tracking devices like the "leave home safe" app became compulsory. People violating the new regulations could be fined or jailed.

"Unity" prevails

In 2019, many would feel the movement was slightly different from the previous ones because it stressed "do not split" and "unity." In other words, people across the political spectrum of democracy supporters joined together to express their dissent and objection to the authorities over the extradition bill, the abuse of police power and the responsibility of the chief executive regarding the bill. But what the protesters wanted – the so called "five demands, not one less" – was never addressed during the whole year.[85]

Amazingly the peaceful group and the radical group did not split; their slogan at the time was "brothers [and sisters] climb mountains together, but by their own efforts." To put it simply, there are many paths to pursue democracy. Just "do not split."[86] The campaign was self-initiated or more correctly it was organised in a democratic way. Anyone could initiate the idea of staging a protest, inside or in the open air; in any of Hong Kong's 18 districts. To the world's surprise, the Hong Kong movement was orderly even though it involved one million and then escalated to two million ordinary citizens. But the scope and scale of the 2019 social movement not only attracted global attention, it also infuriated the Central Government. Clamping down on protesters and maintaining stability became the number one priority. Strategies were rapidly revised and tightened up, with more and more repressive measures in place to nip in the bud any newly sprouted discontent.

Control: Strategies and tactics adopted by the Chinese Communist Party and Hong Kong SAR government

National Security Law, sedition law, and the enactment of Article 23 of Hong Kong Basic Law in 2024

The raid on leading pro-democracy newspaper *Apple Daily* by 200 uniformed policemen and women was horrifying. The action was followed by the arrest, taking away and charging, of senior management and senior editorial staff. Before that, Jimmy Lai, the proprietor, was taken away with chains around his waist and handcuffed. Even that didn't deter staff from continuing to produce the paper; neither did it deter readers from buying the paper. In fact, the circulation surged to a new peak. More importantly, when Jimmy Lai was taken away by the police, the stocks of *Apple Daily's* parent company, the *Next* group, fell. Some opinion leaders advocated buying the parent company's stocks and after several hours of the message spreading on social media, the *Next* stocks bounced back, which showed the genuine support of the Hong Kong public.[87] Then the bank account of *Apple Daily* with a deposit of HK$521 million was frozen. The management and the editorial staff had no choice but to shut down a few days later because they did not have the cash to continue.[88] The day when *Apple Daily* printed its last edition, more than a million copies were sold. The night before, hundreds of readers went to the *Apple Daily* building, turned on their cell-phone lights, held them up, and waved to the staff inside, apparently showing their support and gratitude.[89]

Since 2019, more than 1,000 ordinary citizens have been arrested and charged, among them more than 260 people were under the NSL. Many more people have been arrested, detained, and later released without charge. This pushed a big exodus of professionals who left the city, leaving it short of manpower and reducing the workforce by 5%.[90] Meanwhile, Hong Kong people have become very nervous and dare not speak out even on social media. Even in private events or gatherings, friends and acquaintances tend to be silent or not reveal their position on many issues, especially political topics.

De-radicalisation and re-education for activists such as Tong Ying-kit[91] and Tsang Chi-kin

Tong Ying-kit [92] was the first man jailed under the NSL. In November 2023 a police-promoted TV show featured video of him, recorded inside the prison, in which he expressed remorse and regret. The programme, "National Security Law – the Cornerstone of Prosperity and Stability," released its first episode at the end of November. The 12-episode show was also uploaded to the police YouTube channel and Facebook page. Tong said he was swayed by society's atmosphere. The cameras did not film Tong head on, only showing him at an angle or from the back. It was unclear how police gained access to Tong in custody. Clips of Tong speaking were interspersed with videos of the protests and unrest in 2019.

The same television special featured Tsang Chi-kin, a protester who was shot by police during clashes in 2019 and hid in safe houses for two years before a failed attempt to flee to Taiwan. He was sentenced to three years and 11 months in prison after pleading guilty to charges including rioting and perverting the course of justice. In the two-minute clip, Tsang, a secondary school student during the 2019 protests, said he became a frontline protester because of the "intensifying atmosphere" and that "everyone else was doing the same."[93] The authorities were trying to use the re-education or deradicalisation programme in prisons to alter the story of the movement, pushing the official line that young protesters were swayed by the "society's intensifying atmosphere and doing things that everyone else was doing." They did not admit to any fault in the handling of the unrest, or that it was motivated in any way by impatience at the slow progress towards democracy.

Agnes Chow, once one of the most famous faces of protest in Hong Kong, said she was forced to sign an apology for her past activism to secure her freedom to travel overseas.[94] After she decided not to come back, her mother was summoned and interrogated by police.[95]

Tony Chung has fled Hong Kong to the UK. He was the young activist who once led the very small group advocating Hong Kong independence. Upon arrival in the UK, he talked about his experience after release upon serving a prison sentence, when he should have been free but was repeatedly contacted by police. He was even forced to be a "paid informant" for the National Security police. He said he was fearful because he was summoned and taken in a people carrier to a strange place to be interrogated about his friends' activities. He was forbidden to work even as a waiter for a restaurant supposedly in the Yellow Economy Circle, a cluster of businesses which supported the pro-democracy movement. He was also asked to visit China where he did not feel he would be safe.[96] His mental and physical health both suffered. So Chung asked the National Security police for permission to visit Japan for a few days. When he arrived in Japan, friends helped him to leave for the UK, where he hoped to get political asylum.

Detention of China correspondents

Catherine Wong and Minnie Chan were China correspondents of Hong Kong newspapers who were detained in 2022 and 2023 respectively.[97] Cat Wong was detained in 2022 and supposedly released in mid 2023, but colleagues have not seen her since, and none of her work has been printed since 2023. After the so-called release, some believed she remained in house arrest in Beijing, and her articles were seen once a month. Then after she returned to Hong Kong, she apparently stopped working. She was said to have resigned from her newspaper company *South China Morning Post* (SCMP) in November 2023.[98] Minnie Chan was sent by her newspaper, SCMP to cover a conference regarding defence in October 2023. After that her colleague returned to Hong Kong. According to the SCMP, which responded to a Kyodo News report on her disappearance, she was safe in Beijing dealing with personal matters.[99] Both Catherine and Minnie were regarded as veteran journalists on the SCMP's China desk. Both focused on the diplomatic and military beat, with Minnie said to have People's Liberation Army acquaintances as sources of information.[100] It is unclear why the two journalists were detained, and why the paper they worked for did not appear to seek their release. But the fact that both journalists were detained on the mainland sent a chilling effect to those on the China beat, fearful that they would step on a minefield without knowing it.

Making witnesses out of activists[101]

One of the important witnesses in the trial of Jimmy Lai is activist Lee Yu-hin, who has reportedly said he was "tortured" on many occasions. Inmates heard him screaming from his cell while the 12 Hongkongers arrested in a bid to flee to Taiwan were jailed in mainland China.[102]

'Long-arm administration' or 'extraterritorial rule by law'

Bounties of $1 million were offered for the arrest of eight wanted activists who had already fled Hong Kong.[103] Hong Kong police first offered rewards of HK$1m for information leading to the arrests of five pro-democracy activists.[104] They included Simon Cheng, a former UK consulate employee detained in 2019 in a high-profile case. The others were Frances Hui, Joey Siu, Johnny Fok, and Tony Choi. All were accused of violating the NSL. Other names have followed. The move was condemned by the US and UK where several of the targets live.[105] The police also interrogated and detained the activists' close family members, including parents, siblings, and in-laws. The action further sent a worrying signal to those who remained in Hong Kong. It is not just those activists or politically involved who will be affected, their friends and loved ones will also be involved.

For instance, the wife of trade unionist Lee Cheuk-yan was detained and interrogated when arriving in Hong Kong to visit her husband. Many feared that she would be arrested as she was heavily involved in international union work. Lee's sister-in-law, Marian Tan, was prosecuted for obstruction of justice and was sentenced to six months' jail.[106]

Disappearing bookshops

Many independent bookshops have succumbed to pressure and some chose to close or move voluntarily; to name a few: Mount Zero Books, Have A Nice Stay bookshop, One Punch bookshop, Hunters Bookstore. The intimidation tactics are through numerous visits by different departments investigating whether the shop had followed one rule or another. Mount Zero Books complained that they received complaint letters or were checked by different departments almost every week in the second half of 2023 and more frequently in November and December. So they announced that they would shut down at the end of March 2024.[107] After the announcement, many new customers showed up to take photographs of the bookshop and support the enterprise by buying books and accessories. On Christmas Eve 2023, Mount Zero's owner Sharon Chan and some friends played a Cello Quintet to a big crowd outside the tiny bookshop. Uniformed police officers watched from a distance.[108]

Middle man tactics: The carrot and the stick

This commonly involves a middle man delivering a message, a warning or threat – to shut voluntarily. The idea is to force or influence the concerned institute or media to terminate voluntarily or otherwise co-operate; otherwise legal means, or extra-legal means may be used. The target can be anyone, any institution, creating a sense of insecurity across all walks of life. Journalists are sometimes invited to the National Security Bureau offices in a former hotel in Tin Hau. The setting is decorated with huge banners urging visitors "to preserve national security," "to maintain stability and prosperity." According to journalists who have been summoned, the officers there spoke in Putonghua, with junior officers taking notes of the conversation. The gist of the conversation was "If you don't follow our advice, you have to be responsible and your personal interest will be jeopardised," followed by instructions to postpone publication of a survey, or to cancel a report. On other occasions, the visit may include a friendly gesture: offering a bag of Chinese tea as a token of goodwill.[109]

The Public Opinion Research Institute (PORI) received a visit requesting them to postpone some survey results until after July 1, the national day of Hong Kong and the anniversary of Hong Kong's handover to China. According to sources who are familiar with the situation, PORI later decided not to allow these go-betweens or the National Security Department (NSD) people to visit.[110] PORI instead said that all future interactions should be in writing.[111]

Another technique was to lobby for co-operation and help with united-front work by telling an appealing "Chinese version of the story"[112] China's spy-handlers tried to "turn" outspoken Hong Kong radio host Edmund Wan to tell a good China story. Edmund Wan, also known as "Giggs," said Chinese state security police wanted him to set up a pro-China YouTube channel. Wan was imprisoned for a year because of his involvement in fundraising for young protesters' education and livelihood in Taiwan. After his release he left Hong Kong and moved to Taiwan. He was approached in Taiwan and was advised to stress the good side of China's policy on Hong Kong.[113]

Harassment, intimidation, and visible stalking

Journalists suffered harassment and intimidation. For instance, *Hong Kong Free Press* editors received letters with threatening words and knife blades. Chief editor Tom Grundy guessed it was the same person who sent hate mail not only to him but also to his mother living in England.[114] Several journal-ists reported that they were harassed by surveillance from unidentified per-sons. Some of them were court reporters who covered the *Stand News* trial.[115] According to the HKJA, the journalists in question worked for different organisations. Reportedly there were two unknown men who loitered outside the press room. One of them stayed there for over an hour and attempted to pursue the journalists as they left the courtroom.

Within days of that incident, a reporter for *Hong Kong Free Press* was also followed from her home to her workplace for over an hour by two men with earpieces. Despite efforts to shake them off by changing trains, the two men persisted in tailing the reporter. When one of the men was confronted and questioned by the reporter, he remained silent.[116] The incidents show a deeply worrying trend that Hong Kong journalists not only face legal risks under the NSL but also physical threats to which the Hong Kong authorities turn a blind eye. In December 2023, Ronson Chan, chairperson of HKJA, was followed by two plainclothes Guo An (national security police) inside a church and from the church to outdoors. He confronted one of them with questions while live feeding. The man left swiftly.[117] A press photographer was detained for an ID card check and asked to unlock his phone by police when he went to the Lion Rock to check if there was a protest banner hung up there on 28 September 2023, the ninth anniversary of the Umbrella Movement.[118] Barrister Tim Owen, who happened to be recruited to defend Jimmy Lai of Apple Daily, was barred from having a work visa. While he was appealing this ruling, a relative was video recorded and followed.[119]

Chris Tang, Secretary for Security, has said that Hong Kong has to forgo "marginal advantages" to maintaining a larger good for the benefit of national interest. In other words, Hong Kong's economic interest and whether Hong Kong can continue to play the role as an international information hub and international finance centre are not the main concern.[120]

Last remark

In the next chapter, we shall discuss the protesters' strategy and tactics: how the protesters developed the whole idea of "local identity," grooming each other to become Hongkongers. The protesters used social media to develop the idea of "being water," not looking for a leader to save them. Instead, they initiated and empowered themselves with self-motivated flexibility and fluidity.

Notes

1   Carol P. Lai, *Media in Hong Kong: Press Freedom and Political Change*, London: Routledge, 2007.

2   D. D. Wu, China Says Sino-British Joint Declaration on Hong Kong Is Void, *The Diplomat*, 1 July 2017. On the Hong Kong handover 20th anniversary, China's Foreign Ministry said the document is no longer legally binding, accessed at: https://thediplomat.com/2017/07/%EF%BB%BFchina-says-sino-british-joint -declaration-on-hong-kong-is-void/

3   Xia Baolong, Speech to Hong Kong Elected District Councillors, Xia Baolong Reminds District councillors to Repay Public Support with Concrete Actions, *The Standard*, 22 December 2023, accessed at: https://www.thestandard.com.hk /breaking-news/section/4/211689/Xia-Baolong-reminds-district-councilors-to -repay-public-support-with-concrete-actions

4   "I would rather be ashes than dust!" by Jack London (1876–1916) was quoted in the 1996 Policy Address by Governor Christopher Patten

    ["Hong Kong, it seems to me, has always lived by the author, Jack London's credo:

I would rather be ashes than dust!

    I would rather that my spark should burn out in a brilliant blaze than it should be stifled in dry-rot.

    I would rather be a superb meteor, every atom of me in magnificent glow, than a sleepy and permanent planet.

– by Jack London (1876–1916)]

"Whatever the challenges ahead, nothing should bring this meteor crashing to earth, nothing should snuff out its glow. I hope that Hong Kong will take tomorrow by storm. And when it does, History will stand and cheer." – The 1996 Policy Address by Governor Christopher Francis Patten]

5   Brian Wong, Why Mutually Assured Destruction Rhetoric in Hong Kong Is Dangerous, *The Diplomat*, 6 September 2019. ", Mary Hui, Laam Caau:" The High-Stakes Game That Hong Kong Would Be Destroyed, *Quartz* 30 June, 2022, accessed at https://qz.com/1873189/hong-kong-protesters-gamble-national-secu rity-law-will-backfire-on-china. Simon Shen, Mass Prosecutions Send Chills across Hong Kong's Political Spectrum, *The Diplomat*, 14 April 2021, accessed at: https://thediplomat.com/2021/04/mass-prosecutions-send-chills-across-hong -kongs-political-spectrum/

6   Magnus Ag, Inside Hong Kong's Leaderless Uprising, *The Diplomat*, 24 October 2019, accessed at: https://thediplomat.com/2019/10/inside-hong-kongs-leader less-uprising

7   Hans Tse, Hong Kong Media Mogul Jimmy Lai Ordered Apple Daily Petition Seeking US Sanctions on Beijing, Ex-Publisher Says, *Hong Kong Free Press*, 23 January 2024, accessed at: https://hongkongfp.com/2024/01/23/hong-kong -media-mogul-jimmy-lai-ordered-apple-daily-petition-seeking-us-sanctions-on -beijing-ex-publisher-says/

8   Ibid.

9   Ibid. "Mr Lai was very supportive of young people coming out to resist, and had praised their sacrifice for the homeland," Cheung said, adding that the media mogul wished young people could become devoted readers of Apple Daily.

10 The Beat Generation was a literary subculture movement started by a group of authors whose work explored and influenced American culture and politics in the post-World War II era. Allen Ginsberg's *Howl* (1956), William S. Burroughs' *Naked Lunch* (1959), and Jack Kerouac's *On the Road* (1957) are among the best-known examples of Beat literature. https://en.wikipedia.org/wiki/Beat _Generation

11 Candice Chau, Hong Kong Activist Denies Partaking in Tiananmen Massacre Vigil, Says She Attended Park to Protest Police Ban, *Hong Kong Free Press*, 10 November 2021, accessed at: https://hongkongfp.com/2021/11/10/hong-kong -activist-denies-partaking-in-tiananmen-massacre-vigil-says-she-attended-park -to-protest-police-ban/; Hong Kong: Tiananmen Vigil Convictions an Affront to Human Rights and International Law, Amnesty International, 9 December 2021, accessed at: https://www.amnesty.org/en/latest/news/2021/12/hong-kong-tianan-men-vigil-convictions/

12 Oiwan Lam, Mass Arrests in Hong Kong of Participants in the Pro-Democracy Camp's July 2020 Primaries, Global Voices, 6 January 2021, accessed at: https:// globalvoices.org/2021/01/06/mass-arrests-in-hong-kong-of-participants-in-the -pro-democracy-camps-july-2020-primaries/

13 James Lee, US Lawmakers Introduce Bill to Sanction Hong Kong Judges and Prosecutors; Gov't Slams "Despicable" Intimidation, *Hong Kong Free Press*, 3 November 2023, accessed at: https://hongkongfp.com/2023/11/03/us-lawmakers -introduce-bill-to-sanction-hong-kong-judges-and-prosecutors-govt-slams-des-picable-intimidation/

14 Jessie Pang and James Pomfret, Hong Kong Condemns U.S. Bill Calling for Sanctions on Officials, Reuters, 3 November 2023, accessed at: https://www.reu-ters.com/world/hong-kong-condemns-us-bill-calling-sanctions-officials-2023-11 -03/

15 The World Should Study China's Crushing of Hong Kong's Freedoms, *The Economist*, 24 August 2023, accessed at: https://www.economist.com/china/2023 /08/24/the-world-should-study-chinas-crushing-of-hong-kongs-freedoms

16 Johannes Chan, Hong Kong's National Security Law Turns Three, US-Asia Law Institute, 21 June 2023, accessed at: https://usali.org/usali-perspectives-blog/ hong-kongs-national-security-law-turns-three

17 Interview with Professor Cheng-gang Xu, VOA, 5 August 2023, accessed at: https://www.voachinese.com/a/7211938.html

18 Ibid.

19 Hillary Leung, Hong Kong 47: Democrats "Lacked Willpower" in the Past, Ex-Hospital Authority Union Chief Tells Court, *Hong Kong Free Press*, 23 August 2023, accessed at: https://hongkongfp.com/2023/08/23/hong-kong-47 -democrats-lacked-willpower-in-the-past-ex-hospital-authority-union-chief-tells -court/. Kelly Ho, Hong Kong 47: Benny Tai's "Mutual Destruction" Plan Was "Very Wrong," Democrat Says at National Security Trial, *Hong Kong Free Press*, 17 August 2023, accessed at: https://hongkongfp.com/2023/07/11/hong-kong-47 -benny-tais-mutual-destruction-plan-was-very-wrong-democrat-says-at-national -security-trial/

20 Chen Qingqing, Dozens of Anti-China Figures Including Benny Tai and Joshua Wong Plead Guilty, Sending Deterrent to Secessionists, *Global Times*, 18 August 2022, accessed at: https://www.globaltimes.cn/page/202208/1273278.shtml

21 Candice Chau, Hong Kong Ranks 140th on 2023 Int'l RSF Press Freedom Index below Colombia, Cameroon, *Hong Kong Free Press*, 17 May 2023 https:// hongkongfp.com/2023/05/03/just-in-hong-kong-ranks-140th-on-2023-intl-press -freedom-index-below-colombia-cameroon/ Landmark Hong Kong National Security Trial Opens Two Years after Arrests, Reuters 6 February 2023, accessed at: https://www.asahi.com/ajw/articles/14833031

22 Xinqi Su, Hong Kong's Pro-Democracy Civic Party Disbands after China Cracks Down on Dissent, AFP, 28 December 2023, accessed at: https://www.france24 .com/en/live-news/20231228-jailed-unseated-exiled-hong-kong-opposition -party-shuts-its-doors

23 Hans Tse, Hong Kong's Largest Teachers' Union to Complete Dissolution 2 years after Disbanding, Hong Kong Free Press, 10 November 2023, accessed at: https://hongkongfp.com/2023/11/10/hong-kongs-largest-teachers-union-to-complete-dissolution-2-years-after-disbanding/

24 Ibid.

25 Daniel Payne, Catholic Bishops Call on Hong Kong Government to Release Pro-Democracy Activist Jimmy Lai, *CNA*, 8 November 2023, accessed at: https://www.catholicnewsagency.com/news/255949/catholic-bishops-call-on-hong-kong-government-to-release-pro-democracy-activist-jimmy-lai; Benedict Rogers, The Slow, Insidious Attack on Freedom of Religion in Hong Kong, *The Diplomat*, 17 November 2023, accessed at: https://thediplomat.com/2023/11/the-slow-insidious-attack-on-freedom-of-religion-in-hong-kong/

26 Hong Kong Electoral Reform: LegCo Passes "Patriots" Law, BBC, 27 May 2021, accessed at: https://www.bbc.com/news/world-asia-57236775. Edmond Ng and Sara Cheng, Pro-Beijing "Patriots" Sweep Hong Kong Election with Record Low Turnout, Reuters, December 21 2021, accessed at: https://www.reuters.com/world/china/hong-kong-patriots-only-election-draws-record-low-turnout-2021-12-

27 Louise Delmotte, AP Gets Rare Glimpse of Jailed Hong Kong Pro-Democracy Publisher Jimmy Lai, AP, 13 August 2023, accessed at: https://apnews.com/article/hong-kong-prodemocracy-china-activist-publisher-jimmy-lai-8e03b4415b10754255487d0b0f7b0097

28 Peter Lee, Hong Kong Media Tycoon Jimmy Lai Jailed for 5 Years, 9 Months for Fraud over Apple Daily HQ Lease Violation, *Hong Kong Free Press*, 10 December 2023, accessed at: https://hongkongfp.com/2022/12/10/breaking-hong-kong-media-tycoon-jimmy-lai-jailed-for-5-years-9-months-for-fraud-over-use-of-apple-daily-hq/

29 Kanis Leung, Hong Kong Court Partially Quashes Convictions of Prominent Democracy Activists, Associated Press, 14 August 2023, accessed at: https://time.com/6304508/hong-kong-court-democracy-activists-convictions-jimmy-lai/

30 According to sources familiar with his situation, Jimmy Lai's mobility was further reduced after the AP photo story of his situation in jail was published and went viral globally.

31 *Media in Hong Kong* and Chapter 3 of this book; and comments by Benedict Rogers of Hong Kong Watch in "HongKonger: Jimmy Lai's Extraordinary Struggle for Freedom", film by the Acton Institute, accessed at https://www.youtube.com/watch?v=bRkuv-fOV7k.

32 *Media in Hong Kong*; Chapter 3 of this book.

33 Carol Pui-yee Lai, Interview with Yip Yat-kin, "On the Record" Magazine, Hong Kong Journalists Association. 1996; *Media in Hong Kong*, chapter 3.

34 HongKonger: Jimmy Lai's Extraordinary Struggle for Freedom. *supra* Note 31

35 Newspaper shut down in the wake of cut-throat strategy because *Apple Daily* has taken the major share of Chinese newspaper readership. *Media in Hong Kong*, chapter 3.

36 Cheng Lap, On Media after the 1990s, 27 August 2023, accessed at: https//www.patreon.com/chenglap

37 Gang of four – according to the official Chinese Communist Party media, the four were, Cardinal Zen, Martin Lee, Jimmy Lai, Anson Chan, or Albert Ho; but the names of the four could change at times depending on actual political need. "Gang of Four" "Incited" Unrest in Hong Kong, *China Daily*, 3 November 2019, accessed at: https://www.chinadailyhk.com/articles/228/101/76/1572765209943.html

38 Hong Kong: Jimmy Lai Convicted for Taking Part in Tiananmen Vigil, BBC, 9 December 2021, accessed at: https://www.bbc.com/news/world-asia-59574530

39 Hillary Leung, Hong Kong Media Mogul Jimmy Lai Was "Mastermind and Sponsor" of Foreign Lobbying Efforts, Court Hears, *Hong Kong Free Press*, 4 January 2024, accessed at: https://hongkongfp.com/2024/01/04/hong-kong -media-mogul-jimmy-lai-was-mastermind-and-sponsor-of-foreign-lobbying -efforts-court-hears/

40 Ibid.

41 Tim McLaughlin, Why Beijing Wants Jimmy Lai Locked Up, *The Atlantic*, 6 January 2023, accessed at: https://www.theatlantic.com/international/archive /2023/01/jimmy-lai-chee-ying-hong-kong-prodemocracy-movement/672653/&o =share

42 Ibid.

43 Sebastian Lai, Jimmy Lai's son, lobbied vigorously for his father's release in the US and UK and in December 2023, tried hard to meet the new UK Foreign Secretary, David Cameron, who was said to be on friendly terms with China.

44 According to a 2024 document which listed information collected by HKJA on journalists arrested and sentenced to jail between 2019 and 2024. As journalists and photographers were often injured or arrested while covering the social movement HKJA set up a "fund to protect journalists" and successfully raised funds. After payments by affected journalists, the fund still contained around HK$2.84 million in early 2024.

45 Shibani Mahtan, Hong Kong Prisons Work to Compel Loyalty to China among Young Activists, *The Washington Post*, 8 June 2023, accessed at: https://www .washingtonpost.com/world/interactive/2023/deradicalization-hong-kong -democracy-activists/

46 *Media in Hong Kong*, chapter 2.

47 Ibid.

48 HongKonger: Jimmy Lai's Personal Struggle for Freedom.

49 The Editorial Board, Jimmy Lai's 1,000 Prison Days, *Wall Street Journal*, 25 September 2023. Accessed at https://www.wsj.com/articles/jimmy-lais-1-000 -prison-days-china-ccp-arrest-sentence-kong-truth-freedom. Yasmeen Serhan, Britain Is Failing Citizens Who Are Arbitrarily Jailed Abroad, *Time*, 26 September 2023, accessed at: https://time.com/6317440/uk-failure-abitrary-detention -abroad/

50 HongKonger: Jimmy Lai's Personal Struggle for Freedom.

51 Magnitsky Awards 2023: Honouring the Bravery of the Imprisoned Champions of Democracy, CFHK Foundation, 7 December 2023, accessed at: https://www .thecfhk.org/post/magnitsky-awards-2023-honouring-the-bravery-of-the-impris -oned-champions-of-democracy-1

52 Chen Zifei and Lee Wing Tim, Jailed Hong Kong, Chinese Attorneys Honored with Human Rights Award, *RFA*, 27 November 2023, accessed at: https://www .rfa.org/english/news/china/china-lawyers-awards-11272023160715.html

53 Ibid.

54 According to a source familiar with the situation and who preferred to remain anonymous, Chow received more than 30 letters, which was deemed excessive. So she was punished with solitary confinement for another 18 days for a breach of the rules over which she had no control. She has been punished for several consecutive months for breaking rules. But she continued to urge friends and supporters to send her letters, saying that she is not worried about being punished and kept in solitary confinement without access to TV, books (except religious books) or time in the open air.

55 For Tonyee Chow's solitary confinement see Chow Hang-Tung's Facebook, accessed at: https://www.facebook.com/ChowHangTungClub/photos_albums

56 Ibid.

57 Eunice Lam, NPC Interpretation "Looms If Lai Is Allowed King's Counsel," *The Standard*, 28 November 2022, accessed at: https://www.thestandard.com.hk/section-news/section/11/247715/NPC-interpretation-%27looms-if-Lai-is-allowed-king%27s-counsel%27

58 Samuel Bickett was sentenced to several months in jail for attempting to save a teenager from an attacking policeman in 2019. Other legal firms who specialised in human rights cases have moved out of Hong Kong too. See Shibani Mahtani, American Lawyer Imprisoned in Hong Kong Speaks Out about His Treatment, *The Washington Post*, 12 September 2021, accessed at: https://www.washingtonpost.com/world/asia_pacific/american-lawyer-hongkong-prison/2021/09/11/6e30d66e-f9b2-11eb-911c-524bc8b68f17_story.html

59 Hong Kong: The Four-Year Judicial Ordeal of Swiss Photojournalist Who Covered a 2019 Demonstration, Reporters Sans Frontieres (RSF), 23 September 2023, accessed at: https://rsf.org/en/hong-kong-four-year-judicial-ordeal-swiss-photojournalist-who-covered-2019-demonstration

60 The author was among the audience at the court hearings for nearly 40 days when Chung stood as a witness at Wan Chai regional court on this first sedition case involving news media.

61 In the *Stand News* case, former chief editor Chung Pui-kuen has been detained for 11 months while his acting chief editor Patrick Lam has been detained for 10 months. The judge of the SN case pronounced in court that he would postpone delivering the verdict 30 days after the verdict of "Fast Beat" seditious case from the High Court was delivered in the next March or later.

62 Chat with a veteran journalist who is familiar with the incident and preferred to remain anonymous because of fear of reprisals, October 2023. Timothy McLaughlin and Rachel Cheung, A Eulogy for the Free Press, *The Atlantic*, 24 June 2021, accessed at: https://www.theatlantic.com/international/archive/2021/06/hong-kong-apple-daily/619278/. Lea Mok, Ex-Chief Editor of Hong Kong Outlet Stand News Planned to Step down after Apple Daily Closure, Court Hears, *Hong Kong Free Press*, 11 January 2023, accessed at: https://hongkongfp.com/2023/01/11/ex-chief-editor-of-hong-kong-outlet-stand-news-planned-to-step-down-after-apple-daily-closure-court-hears/; Lea Mok, Hong Kong Police Began Archiving over 300 Stand News Articles Days after Apple Daily Arrests and Raid, Court Hears, *Hong Kong Free Press*, 4 November 2022, accessed at: https://hongkongfp.com/2022/11/04/hong-kong-police-began-archiving over-300-stand-news-articles-days-after-apple-daily-arrests-and-raid-court-hears/

63 See article in *The Atlantic* cited above.

64 Lea Mok, Hong Kong Outlet Stand News Name Cards Showed Reporters' Political Stance, Prosecutor Argues in Sedition Trial, *Hong Kong Free Press*, 27 January 2023, accessed at: https://hongkongfp.com/2023/01/27/design-of-stand-news-name-cards-shows-hong-kong-outlets-political-stance-prosecutor-argues-in-sedition-trial/ . Brian Wong, Hong Kong National Security Law: Children's Books Aimed at Inciting Separatism and Hatred towards Mainland China, Prosecutors Say, *SCMP*, 5 July 2022, accessed at: https://www.scmp.com/news/hong-kong/law-and-crime/article/3184218/hong-kong-national-security-law-childrens-books-aimed. Lea Mok, Satirical Images and Protest-Related Articles Questioned in Sedition Trial against Hong Kong Outlet *Stand News*, *Hong Kong Free Press*, 26 January 2023, accessed at: https://hongkongfp.com/2023/01/26/

political-comics-and-protest-related-articles-questioned-in-sedition-trial-against
-hong-kong-outlet-stand-news/

65 According to journalists who covered the 2019 social movement and preferred to remain anonymous for fear of reprisal, they got the impression that the police and the authorities were targeting them, in particular when they refused to move back or leave the confrontation spot. For example, Ronson Chan, then an executive committee member of the Hong Kong Journalists Association, had tear gas fired directly at his face. Almost all photographers at confrontations between protesters and police had bodily injuries caused by tear gas, rubber bullets, bean bag bullets, or water cannons.

66 Zen Soo, Hong Kong Police Offer Rewards for Arrests of 8 Pro-Democracy Activists Who Live Abroad, Associated Press, 3 July 2023, accessed at: https:// apnews.com/article/national-security-law-arrests-reward-05e6c0e715de228ed51 879fc20fee381 . Saša Petricic, "Palpable Fear": 3 Years after Beijing Tightened Control, Hong Kongers Speak in Cautious Whispers, CBC News, 28 June 2023, accessed at: https://www.cbc.ca/news/hong-kong-china-national-security-law-1 .6890220

67 *Stand News*: Independent Outlet to Close after Senior Staff Arrested, BBC, 29 December 2021, accessed at: https://www.bbc.com/news/world-asia-59807734

68 Fung Kim-ki and pan-democrats alike to adopt a "compromise and criticize" strategy, which was lamented and rejected by young politicians such as Winnie Yu. Hilary Leung, Hong Kong 47: Democrats "Lacked Willpower" in the Past, Ex-Hospital Authority Union Chief Tells Court, *Hong Kong Free Press*, 23 August 2023, accessed at: https://hongkongfp.com/2023/08/23/hong-kong-47 -democrats-lacked-willpower-in-the-past-ex-hospital-authority-union-chief-tells -court/

69 Chat with veteran journalist who is familiar with the situation and preferred to remain anonymous for fear of reprisal, November 2022.

70 Kelly Ho, "Distorting the Truth": Ex-Reporter Rejects Police Claims of "Biased Live-Stream" during Yuen Long Attacks, *Hong Kong Free Press*, 27 August 2020, accessed at: https://hongkongfp.com/2020/08/27/distorting-the-truth-ex -reporter-rejects-police-claims-of-biased-live-stream-during-yuen-long-attacks/

71 Hillary Leung, Hong Kong 47: Activist Gwyneth Ho Believed in Vetoing the Budget during Her Journalist Days, Court Hears, *Hong Kong Free Press*, 20 July 2023, accessed at: https://hongkongfp.com/2023/07/20/hong-kong-47-activist -gwyneth-ho-believed-in-vetoing-the-budget-during-her-journalist-days-court -hears/

72 Primrose Riordan and Chan Ho-him, She Was Loved for Standing up to China. She May Die in Jail, *Financial Times*, 23 June 2022, accessed at: https://www.ft .com/content/439fb015-8fc7-4d2d-9c7f-8764863090ae

73 Mary Hui, The Journalist Who Livestreamed the Hong Kong Protests' Darkest Moment Is Now a Dissident behind Bars, *Quartz*, 30 March 2021, accessed at: https://qz.com/1987247/a-journalist-who-covered-hong-kong-protests-now -faces-life-in-jail

74 Amelia Loi, Tens of Thousands of Hong Kongers Struggle to Adapt to Life in the UK: Survey, *RFA Mandarin*, 5 February 2023, accessed at: https://www.rfa.org /english/news/china/hongkong-uk-adaptation-02052023121250.html. Monika Pitrelli, Thousands of People Are Leaving Hong Kong – and Now It's Clear Where They're Going, CNBC, 27 May 2022, accessed at: https://www.cnbc .com/2022/05/27/people-are-leaving-hong-kong-and-here-is-where-they-are -going.html. John Power, Hong Kongers Fleeing China's Crackdown Denied Pension Savings, *Al Jazeera*, 9 May 2023, accessed at: https://www.aljazeera

.com/economy/2023/5/9/hong-kongers-fleeing-chinas-crackdown-denied-pen-sion-savings

75 Tom Grundy, Ten Arrests as Hong Kong Police Deploy in Force on 4th Anniv. of Yuen Long Mob Attacks, *Hong Kong Free Press*, 22 July 2023, accessed at: https://hongkongfp.com/2023/07/22/ten-arrests-as-hong-kong-police-deploy-in-force-on-4th-anniv-of-yuen-long-mob-attacks/

76 Ibid.

77 Shifting Narratives: From "Violent Attack" to "Gang Fight" – How the Official Account of the Yuen Long Mob Attack Changed, *Hong Kong Free Press*, 21 July 2021, accessed at: https://hongkongfp.com/2021/07/21/from-violent-attack-to-gang-fight-how-the-official-account-of-the-yuen-long-mob-attack-changed-over-a-year/

78 Arrest of Stand News Senior Editorial Staff: Vivian Wang, Hong Kong police raid office of pro-democracy news site and arrest 7, NYT 28 December 2021. Accessed at: https://www.nytimes.com/2021/12/29/world/asia/hong-kong-stand-news-arrest.html

79 Hong Kong: Journalists on Trial and Tiananmen Massacre Commentators Arrested, BBC, 4 July 2023, accessed at: https://www.youtube.com/watch?v=WE5PUMFMyms

80 Tears of Ronson Chan – Hong Kong Commercial Radio morning programme, "On a Clear Day" – Live Interview with Ronson Chan on the Police Raid and Shut down of *Stand News*. See Ronson Chan, Ex-senior Staff of Stand News to Lose His Position as HKJA Chairman If He Fails to Find a Job in 3 months, *DimSum Daily*, accessed at: https://www.dimsumdaily.hk/ronson-chan-ex-senior-staff-of-stand-news-to-lose-his-position-as-hkja-chairman-if-he-fails-to-find-a-job-in-3-months/. Timothy McLaughlin, I'm Afraid That I Cannot Be a Journalist Anymore, *The Atlantic*, 19 February 2022, accessed at: https://www.theatlantic.com/international/archive/2022/02/hong-kong-china-stand-news/622092/

81 Tommy Walker, Is Hong Kong's Last Pro-Democracy Newspaper Doomed?, *VOA*, 3 June 2021, accessed at: https://www.voanews.com/a/press-freedom_hong-kongs-last-pro-democracy-newspaper-doomed/6206579.html

82 Judith Pernin and Eric Florence, 1989–2019: Perspectives on June 4th from Hong Kong, *CEFC*, 2019, accessed at: https://www.cefc.com.hk/article/1989-2019-perspectives-on-june-4th-from-hong-kong/

83 Jude Blanchette, How Close Is Hong Kong to a Second Tiananmen? *Foreign Policy*, 14 August 2019, accessed at: https://foreignpolicy.com/2019/08/14/how-close-is-hong-kong-to-a-second-tiananmen/

84 Brian Kern/Kong Tsung-gan, The Police Sieges of CUHK and PolyU Four Years On: A Historic Watershed, 12 November 2023, accessed at: https://briankernkongtsunggan.substack.com/p/the-police-sieges-of-cuhk-and-polyu. Protests, Siege Continue in Hong Kong as China Rails at Passage of US Bill, *RFA*, 20 November 2019. accessed at https://www.rfa.org/english/news/china/hongkong-siege-11202019123643.html

85 Five demands, not one less. The slogan "five demands, not one less" is explained in *Hong Kong Protest Movement Data Archive: Glossary*, accessed at https://hongkongfp.com/hong-kong-protest-movement-data-archive-glossary/: The five demands were:

(1) full withdrawal of the extradition bill,
(2) retracting the characterisation of the protests as riots,
(3) amnesty for all arrested protesters,
(4) universal suffrage for the Chief Executive and the Legislative Council, and
(5) an independent investigation into allegations of police brutality.

The first two demands, alongside two other demands: that Carrie Lam step down and for the release of all injured student protesters, were first shown on a placard displayed by Leung Ling-kit (梁凌杰) before he fell to his death on 15 June 2019. The Civic Human Rights Front took on his idea, turning "release all injured student protesters" to "discharge all arrested protesters" and added a fifth demand, formulating the first version of the "five demands." On 1 July 2019, some protesters stormed into the Legislative Council Complex and replaced "Carrie Lam steps down" with a call for universal suffrage in their declaration. This then became widely adopted by other protesters as the new version of the five demands, accessed at: https://hongkongfp.com/hong-kong-protest-movement-data-archive -glossary/

86 Translated as "brothers climb mountains together, but by their own efforts," it means that peaceful and valiant protesters are like brothers. Although they climb the mountain by their own efforts and their own ways, they share the same goal of democracy and have to each exert their own efforts, accessed at: https://hong-kongfp.com/hong-kong-protest-movement-data-archive-glossary/

87 Kenji Kawase and Michelle Chan, Hong Kongers Buy Stock and Newspapers to Support Apple Daily, *Nikkei*, 11 August 2020, accessed at: https://asia.nikkei .com/Business/Media-Entertainment/Hong-Kongers-buy-stock-and-newspapers -to-support-Apple-Daily2

88 John Cheng, Felix Tam, and Iain Marlow, Apple Daily to Suspend Paper If Hong Kong Accounts Stay Frozen, *Bloomberg*, 21 June 2021, accessed at: https://www .bloomberg.com/news/articles/2021-06-21/hong-kong-s-apple-daily-to-decide -monday-on-shutting-down-paper

89 Jessie Pang, Hong Kong Pro-Democracy Paper Apple Daily to Print Last Edition on Thursday, Reuters, 24 June 2021, accessed at: https://www.reuters.com/world /asia-pacific/hong-kong-police-arrest-apple-daily-columnist-under-security-law -media-2021-06-23/

90 Irene Chan, Over Half of Hong Kong Professionals Considering Leaving the City within 5 Years, Survey Finds, *Hong Kong Free Press*, 4 October 2023, accessed at: https://hongkongfp.com/2023/10/04/over-half-of-hong-kong-professionals -considering-leaving-the-city-within-5-years-survey-finds/

91 Hillary Leung, Man Jailed under Security Law Says He was Swayed By Society's Atmosphere in Hong Kong Police-Promoted TV Show, *HKFP*, 14 December 2023, accessed at: https://hongkongfp.com/2023/12/14/man-jailed-under-secu-rity-law-says-he-was-swayed-by-societys-atmosphere-in-hong-kong-police-pro-moted-tv-show/

92 Holmes Chan, Inside the Surreal Trial of the "Most Benevolent Terrorist in the World," *Vice*, 20 September 2021, accessed at: https://www.vice.com/en/article /93y47p/hong-kong-national-security-trial-tong-ying-kit.

93 Hans Tse, Hong Kong Student Shot during 2019 Protest Featured as Remorseful in Police-Promoted TV Special, *Hong Kong Free Press*, 5 December 2023, accessed at: https://hongkongfp.com/2023/12/05/hong-kong-student-shot-during -2019-protest-featured-as-remorseful-in-police-promoted-tv-special/

94 Rebecca Choong Wilkins, Inside Hong Kong's Secretive Tactics to Muzzle, Discredit Dissent, *Bloomberg*, 11 December 2023, accessed at: https://www .bloomberg.com/news/articles/2023-12-11/inside-hong-kong-s-secretive-tactics -to-muzzle-discredit-dissent

95 Hans Tse, Parents of Hong Kong Self-Exiled Activist Agnes Chow Questioned By Police – Local Media, *Hong Kong Free Press*, 29 December 2023, accessed at: https://hongkongfp.com/2023/12/29/parents-of-hong-kong-self-exiled-activ-ist-agnes-chow-questioned-by-police-local-media/

96 Hong Kong Democracy Activist Tony Chung Flees to UK to Seek Asylum, AFP, 29 December 2023, accessed at: https://www.france24.com/en/live-news/20231229-hong-kong-democracy-advocate-seeks-asylum-in-britain

97 Hong Kong Journalist Goes Missing Following Business Trip to Beijing, *Kyodo News*, 1 December 2023, accessed at: https://english.kyodonews.net/news/2023/12/40f577e22e31-hong-kong-journalist-goes-missing-following-business-trip-to-beijing.html

98 According to several sources at the SCMP, Catherine was said to have returned to Hong Kong, but no colleagues have seen her back in the office.

99 Hong Kong Journalist Goes Missing Following Business Trip to Beijing, *Kyodo News*, 1 December 2023, accessed at: https://english.kyodonews.net/news/2023/12/40f577e22e31-hong-kong-journalist-goes-missing-following-business-trip-to-beijing.html

100 According to sources at the SCMP who preferred to remain anonymous for fear of reprisal, December 2023.

101 Hong Kong Tycoon's Lawyers Appeal to UN Over Witness Torture Accusation, Reuters, 5 January 2024, accessed at: https://www.reuters.com/world/china/hong-kong-tycoons-lawyers-appeal-un-over-witness-torture-accusation-2024-01-04/ and Jimmy Lai's National Security Law trial: Urgent appeal filed with United Nations raising grave concerns over the treatment of prosecution witness, Andy Li, and the reliability of his evidence against Jimmy Lai, *Doughty Street Chambers*, 4 January 2024, accessed at:https://www.doughtystreet.co.uk/news/jimmy-lais-national-security-law-trial-urgent-appeal-filed-united-nations-raising-grave

102 Shibani Mahtani, Witness against Hong Kong Media Mogul Was Mistreated, Post Examination Finds, *The Washington Post*, 17 December 2023, accessed at: https://www.washingtonpost.com/world/2023/12/17/jimmy-lai-trial-witness-treatment-hong-kong/

103 Hong Kong Police Offer Bounties for 8 Prominent Overseas Activists, AFP, 3 July 2023, accessed at: https://www.france24.com/en/live-news/20230703-hong-kong-police-offer-bounties-for-8-prominent-overseas-activists-1

104 Jojo Man and Amelia Loi, Hong Kong Police Arrest Five for Helping Exiled Activists, *RFA*, 6 July 2023, accessed at: https://www.rfa.org/english/news/china/hong-kong-five-arrested-07062023141455.html

105 Kelly Ng, Hong Kong Offers HK$1m Bounties on Five Overseas Activists, BBC, 15 December 2023, accessed at: https://www.bbc.com/news/world-asia-china-67724230

106 Edward Cho and Jessie Pang, Hong Kong Court Jails Sister of Veteran Labour Activist for Six Months, Reuters, 21 December 2023, accessed at: https://www.reuters.com/world/china/hong-kong-court-jails-sister-veteran-labour-activist-six-months-2023-12-21/

107 Mount Zero Books IG post, 5 December 2023 accessed at: https://www.instagram.com/mountzerobooks/p/C0dttxZv9FG/?img_index=1; Carol Lai, [港呢D] 見山又是山, *RFA Cantonese*, 2 January 2024, accessed at: https://www.youtube.com/watch?v=1z1Ys5Kf7E8

108 Ibid.

109 Visits by National Security Department (NSD) officer to some institute's office and offered tea as a souvenir; others may be summoned to NSD in a hotel in Tin Hau. So NSD personnel were nicknamed "Tin Hau" which meant they were from the district Tin Hau. In fact, Tin Hau also referred to the 'almighty goddess' who helped the fishing community to overcome a storm if they faithfully prayed and made offerings to the goddess.

110 According to sources who preferred to be anonymous and who are familiar with the situation.

111 Kanis leung, Leading Hong Kong Pollster to Stop Releasing Poll Results on Some Sensitive Topics, Associated Press (AP), 27 July 2023, accessed at: https:// apnews.com/article/hong-kong-independent-pollster-shrinking-freedoms-24a 47d420e65d5e4b229309809f4a5e2

112 Su Xinqi, The Shadowy Messengers Delivering Threats to Hong Kong Civil Society, AFP, 21 February 2022, accessed at: https://hongkongfp.com/2022/02 /21/the-shadowy-messengers-delivering-threats-to-hong-kong-civil-society/; Rebecca Choong Wilkins, Inside Hong Kong's Secretive Tactics to Muzzle, Discredit Dissent, *Bloomberg,* 11 December 2023, accessed at: https://www .bloomberg.com/news/articles/2023-12-11/inside-hong-kong-s-secretive-tactics -to-muzzle-discredit-dissent

113 Ching Fung, China's Spy-handlers Tried to "Turn" Outspoken Hong Kong Radio Host, *RFA Cantonese*, 2 October 2023, accessed at: https://www.rfa.org/english/ news/china/giggs-10022023143717.html

114 Police Launch Investigation after Threatening Letters Sent to Hong Kong Free Press Staff, *Hong Kong Free Press*, 4 October 2017. Accessed at https://hong-kongfp.com/2017/10/04/police-launch-investigation-threatening-letters-sent -hong-kong-free-press-staff/ Author chat with Tom Grundy, who reported that he and his mother received warning letters with a knife blade enclosed.

115 Hong Kong: Journalists Complain of Being Stalked While Reporting on Court Cases, *Practice Source*, undated, accessed at: https://practicesource.com/hong -kong-free-press-journalists-complain-of-being-stalked-while-reporting-on-court -cases/

116 Hong Kong: HKFP Journalists Report Stalking and Intimidation, IFJ, 4 April 2023, accessed at: https://www.ifj.org/media-centre/news/detail/category/press -freedom/article/hong-kong-hkfp-journalists-report-stalking-and-intimidation

117 Ronson Chan, Hong Kong Journalists Association chairperson was followed by suspicious people, apparently police or Guo An (national security officer). Chan managed to catch up with one and make a live stream on his own Facebook page on 10 December 2023, accessed at: http://www.facebook.com/ronsingchan

118 *Hong Kong Free Press* photographer Kyle Lam was detained for several hours when he went to the Lion Rock to see if anyone dared to put up a banner or laser light on top of the mountain.

119 Amy Hawkins, Hong Kong Lecture By British Barrister Linked to Jimmy Lai Trial Cancelled, *The Guardian*, 14 November 2023, accessed at: https://www.the-guardian.com/world/2023/nov/14/hong-kong-lecture-by-british-barrister-linked -to-jimmy-lai-trial-cancelled

120 Michael Shum, They're Like the Mafia and Triads, *The Standard*, 6 November 2023, accessed at: https://www.thestandard.com.hk/section-news/section/4 /257549/%27They%27re-like-the-Mafia-and-triads%27

4 Media, Internet, and the Civil Movement in Hong Kong

Control and protest (part 2: protest)

In the previous chapter, we talked about how the authorities tried to suppress the protests by legal and extra-judicial means, using the NSL, the draconian sedition law, and the offering of bounties for the arrest of activists residing overseas. However, these were only the culmination of a period of escalation and intimidation, mostly deployed when the unrest had already died down. All too often, the government chose to provoke opposition rather than make any attempt to address people's grievances.

In the very beginning only a few thousand people took to the streets, followed by several hundred thousand, and then one million people on 12 June 2019 when the government tried to have the second reading of the extradition bill, which would have allowed the government to send suspects to China for national security trials. Even though the widespread opposition to the bill was loud and unequivocal, the authorities resorted to violent tactics to combat public opposition, dispersing protesters with tear gas, rubber bullets, bean bag projectiles, water cannon and other weapons which injured many. And then two million people took to the streets to condemn police brutality, and demand an investigation of the apparent abuse of power. This joined other demands: dropping charges against detained protesters, removing the label of "riots" on the protests and universal suffrage for Hong Kong. However, all these five demands fell on deaf ears. The government was reluctant to take heed of any different opinions. Hostility and alienation mounted until the July 21 incident in Yuen Long, a turning point which for many Hongkongers conclusively demonstrated that the police force was an enemy.[1] Similarly, the government's continuing neglect of legitimate grievances and deafness to opposition voices was taken to demonstrate that the HKSAR Chief Executive was not accountable to the Hong Kong people, but took her orders from the central government of China. There was, accordingly, no room for negotiation and compromise.

Characteristics of the 2019 movement

The onset of the 2019 movement, after years in which opposition had routinely been frustrated and marginalised, surprised many. There are several

DOI: 10.4324/9781003150244-4

characteristics of the 2019 civil movements. Firstly, protesters were motivated by a set of five demands, which focused on police powers, the unrepresentative political system, and the absence of progress towards democracy promised in the Sino-British Joint Declaration. Secondly, there was no prominent leader; the protesters were self-mobilised and technologically literate, enabling the decentralisation of authority in the movement. Thirdly, by displaying a high level of solidarity unseen in previous protests, the self-motivated protesters staged highly imaginative and innovative protests by using different forms of expression, engaging the young, middle-aged, and elderly across all walks of life, further enhancing the momentum for escalation and radicalisation.

Previous research findings indicated that despite some basic continuities with past trajectories, political activism had undergone a profound evolution under the increasingly authoritarian regime in post-handover Hong Kong.[2] The movement in 2019 was unprecedented, in demographic terms by covering a wide range of participants, and in initially deploying only law-abiding behaviours. There was no arson, looting, or destruction of public utilities until the protesters were confronted with escalating violence and increasingly sophisticated and life-threatening weapons. Then they started to change to what they called "resolved in their own ways (Si Liao)" including using valiant or violent means.[3] Research has shown that this mass action sprang both directly and indirectly from sympathy for the protests' objectives.[4]

In this chapter, we shall attempt to discuss

1. The characteristics/philosophy of "be like water"; the protesters' use of social media such as Telegram and Lihkg, Facebook, and X (formerly known as Twitter), to provide flexibility, fluidity, and spontaneity, engaging ordinary people's participation.
2. The evolution of teenage "dissenting youth" or the "burnt generation" – the identity of which was apparently awakened through their vision to pursue democracy. They resented the pan-democrats' decade-long compromising strategy, which had produced no progress, were disillusioned with the Chinese authorities, and rejected Chinese identity for a newly consolidated identity of "Hongkonger." This should not be confused with the idea of "Hong Kong independence" which was actually very rare and insignificant.
3. In the course of this enormous general uprising involving up to millions of protesters, the role of the two leading democratic media — the traditional newspaper *Apple Daily* and newly emerged digital media, *Stand News,* should not be underestimated. The authorities have branded these two media as the "ringleader" and its "Plan B".

The essence of the "be like water" movement in 2019: Not "Hong Kong independence" advocacy

The 2019 protests had nothing to do with the idea of an "independent Hong Kong." The pro-Beijing and Chinese Communist Party (CCP) media orchestrated this idea to give the Hong Kong authorities an excuse for clamping down on the movement.[5] Most Hong Kong people never expected to enjoy any nationality other than "Chinese". The passport offered by the departing colonial power was a British National Overseas (BNO) passport which conferred no right of abode in the UK. It could only be used as a travel document before and after 1997.[6] In the wake of the imposition of the National Security Law in 2020, British policy changed, giving Hong Kong BNO passport holders the right to stay in the UK for five years and eventually become full residents.[7]

Hong Kong as a new "ethnic group"

The term "Chinese" is used for everyone on the mainland, even though many provinces have distinctive languages, cultures and ethnic backgrounds. The identification of Hong Kong as a special place whose inhabitants regarded themselves as "Hongkongers" turned a new page in Hong Kong's history. This unprecedented move, after 90% or more of the city's inhabitants identified themselves as "Chinese" even under British colonial rule, made the 2019 civil movement different from other movements in 2014 and 2012. It also infuriated the central government. Highlighting this idea may enhance our understanding of the real objectives of the movement in 2019 and the democracy movement's logic — which was, in essence, about affirming Hong Kong's identity as distinct from mainland China's socialist system, and reclaiming Hong Kong's capitalist values: freedom, rule of law and fair play in a market economy. The democracy movement participants regarded this as a "revolution of the times."[8] Unfortunately the mere act of wearing a T-shirt with the resulting slogan "reclaim Hong Kong, revolution of the era" is now a crime and earned a jail sentence in 2023.[9]

Decentralizing decision making in a civil movement

In 2019 there was no "prominent activist" leading the movement; protesters used what they called "be water" tactics, filling any protest site or indoor venue, then moving swiftly when faced with threats from police or gangsters. To a large extent, this "leaderless" tactic was an alternative to the decade-long democratic movement led by the pan-democrats. Armed with decentralised and spontaneous decision-making, protesters shocked the city with unfiltered live feeds on the internet and traditional TV. Even the protesters themselves may not have envisaged the full impact of this.[10] Subsequently both traditional and digital media were targeted by the authorities, and regarded as a target/ scapegoat to be destroyed. The official line is that the 2019 movement was a tactic used by foreign powers to threaten the national security of both Hong Kong and China. The Chinese authorities prefer to ignore the fact that it was, in fact a general uprising supported by more than a third of Hong Kong residents.

On the protest front, the protesters had learnt from previous movements; they were deeply disappointed with the role of the pan-democrats leading the democratic movement and making no progress.[11] More importantly, the pan-democrats had joined the chorus on the "reunification of a greater China." They rejoiced in being Chinese and in Hong Kong's return to China in 1997, although they often reiterated and believed that Hong Kong was returning to China armed with a promise of democracy in 2007 and beyond.

According to an annual survey of Hong Kong people's sentiment towards the Central Government since the handover, the number of Hong Kong people who identified with mainland China reached a record low in 2019.[12] The Public Opinion Programme at the University of Hong Kong interviewed more than 1,000 residents in mid-2019 after two million people had joined a march calling for the withdrawal of the controversial extradition bill.[13] The number of people who identified as "Hongkonger" was at its highest since 1997, while those feeling proud of being a citizen of China had dropped from over one-third the previous year to around one-quarter that year.[14] The survey, conducted after the two major protest marches against the extradition bill, clearly reflected the impact of the issue on Hong Kong citizens' identity and feelings towards the handover of sovereignty. In-depth analysis showed that the younger the respondents, the less likely they felt proud of becoming a national of China, and also the more negative they were towards China's policies on Hong Kong. Critics had raised concerns over the risk of residents being extradited to mainland China, which lacked human rights protections. The bill was suspended following mass protests, but the government was reluctant to withdraw it entirely.[15]

Increase in identifying as Chinese after National Security law passed

However in 2022, two years after the imposition of the national security bill, the number of Hong Kong adults identifying as "Chinese" was the highest since 2018. Analysts said the change in identity could be related to the emigration wave and a changing outlook among those who stayed in Hong Kong. "In order to survive, prosper and thrive… you have to adjust your mindset," was a popular view. Although "Hongkonger" remained the most commonly held identity among respondents, the survey found that more residents aged 30 or above identified as "Chinese" in recent years.[16] As Hong Kong's democratic movement reached a low point, the researcher said that many with strong feelings against mainland China or the CCP had already left the city.[17]

On the political front, unsurprisingly, with the general disappointment with the pan-democratic politicians as becoming too close to Beijing and its Liaison Office in Hong Kong, while making no progress towards democracy, the democracy movement in 2019 became self-organising and dispensed with the leading role and direction of a prominent leader. The protesters called this arrangement "without a main stage." It was possible due to the popularity of the internet and swift use of apps and global platforms. In the wake of this revelation, the protesters' use of social media to develop the idea of "be like water" decentralised decision-making. They initiated and empowered themselves with flexibility of strategy and fluidity of tactics by using votes via social media to determine when, what and how a protest should be conducted, and how to get things done. At times, the discussion of direction and way of doing things could be rigorous, tedious, and time consuming. It could also be dangerous. Undercover government agents and other opponents of the movement lurked on the internet.

Protest: Strategies and tactics adopted by protesters and the media

The motto "be water, my friend" – a catchphrase used to describe a sublime level of martial arts by movie star Bruce Lee – was adopted by the protesters from the summer of 2019. The essence of the motto was: be flexible and ready to move, filling any vessel (protest venue) with your presence just like water, but disperse swiftly so as not to get caught or assaulted when a clampdown was imminent and about to turn violent.[18] In the wake of that motto, there was a sudden surge of usage on Lihkg (something like Reddit) and Telegram. The use of social media was mainly for the sake of cybersecurity and to avoid government surveillance.[19] The apparently ad hoc way of doing things, for example engaging in protest events without a planned time and venue, was an effective way of avoiding suppression and making it harder for the authorities to track down participants.

The deployment of media to compete on the battlefield of public opinion, and the use of social media to avoid surveillance and to swiftly communicate, discuss, organise and mobilise, were big concerns among protesters. To a large extent, the movement involved a number of anonymous organisers, hundreds and thousands of anonymous protesters and an enormous number of participants, many protesting for the first time.[20]

Completely different from the Umbrella Movement in 2014, the protesters had become more mature and could engage in a "leaderless" movement which would enable them to voice their grievances without following someone else's instructions. The reason was mainly to avoid being pinned down by the authorities and targeted in a subsequent purge. To a certain extent, activists had also lost trust in conventional politicians. The movement spread to the

18 districts and took on different forms, such as peaceful "lunch with you" in a mall to shout slogans of "liberate Hong Kong, revolution of our times," "sing with you," "Hallelujah," or playing the music of the song "Glory to Hong Kong" which later became an apparent "Hong Kong anthem" in shopping malls; "human chain" (holding hands or linking arms in school uniforms in front of a secondary school to demonstrate solidarity),[21] or using torch lights to connect a chain of light up the Lion Rock, a mountain which represented Hong Kong people's spirit.[22]

Framing a separatist movement by disinformation: 'Hong Kong independence'

During the course of local protests, the authorities constructed an "independence" myth for the Hong Kong protests through information operations framing protesters as a separatist movement. According to academic research, since August 2019 China's information operations on Hong Kong protests have unfurled internationally. This was brought to light after a number of social media platforms, including Twitter and Facebook, discovered the existence of coordinated network activities by China spreading disinformation about Hong Kong protests. The aim of these operations was to undermine the protest movement's legitimacy.[23]

Follow-up research and data analysis by the University of Hong Kong Media Centre on content from 640,000 Twitter user accounts which had posted Hong Kong-related news since June 2019 found that about 20% of the 640,000 Twitter users were robots.[24] The research found that inside China's Great Firewall, disinformation spread on social media aimed to construct a "pro-Hong Kong independence" frame for Hong Kong's anti-extradition movement. Hong Kong protests were labelled acts of "pro-Hong Kong independence" by China's social media news outlet Weibo.[25]

Users who made pro-protest comments outside the Great Firewall on Twitter, Facebook, and Instagram, once they were spotted by mainland Chinese netizens and reported on Chinese social media platforms, could face tremendous pressure, especially if they had business connections with China. Even Hong Kong tycoon Li Ka-shing was no exception. He had advocated in a political advertisement for the peaceful resolution of the current conflicts. However, any views that criticised both the protesters and the government were considered politically incorrect by the Chinese authorities.[26]

Furthermore, pro-Beijing violent acts were praised on mainland Chinese social media as heroic. Lennon Walls, public art spaces which had been set up spontaneously by local residents in many districts for free expression, were labelled "pro-Hong Kong independence" sites. Taking action to destroy the walls was depicted as an upright action. After August 2019, many protesters were attacked by pro-Beijing individuals when they were putting up posters near Lennon Walls.[27]

However, "Hong Kong independence" was not even on the agenda of the Hong Kong protesters. The five demands of the protests were complete withdrawal of the extradition bill, an independent investigation into police operations, the dropping of all riot charges against the protesters, amnesty for arrested protesters, and universal suffrage to choose the Hong Kong Legislature and Hong Kong SAR Chief Executive. None of these demands included calls for Hong Kong independence.

The emergence of the 'pro-Hong Kong independence' framework

Initial findings strongly suggest that the CCP and state media apparatus played a key role in spreading information framing the protests as a "pro-Hong Kong independence" movement. This was intended to persuade Chinese public opinion that the discontent was part of a separatist political plot to undermine "the integrity of Chinese territory," a phrase repeatedly used on Chinese social and news media.[28]

On 21 July 2019, the Civil Human Rights Front organised a march from Causeway Bay to Wan Chai on Hong Kong Island. After the peaceful protest, a large number of protesters marched on to the Beijing Liaison Office in the Western District. The same night, a large group of pro-Beijing gangsters rushed into the Yuen Long Mass Transit Railway station, attacking protesters and other passengers. Many were seriously injured.

The following day the term "pro-Hong Kong independence," previously censored, appeared multiple times on Weibo.[29] Beijing's state and CCP affiliated media outlets ran commentaries on the protest outside the Beijing Liaison Office and in particular framed the staining of the national emblem as a "pro-Hong Kong independence" act. The once politically sensitive and loaded term has since been widely used on Chinese social media.

According to the research finding, 13% of the posts which contained the keyword "Hong Kong independence" were directly re-posted from CCP media *People's Daily* and *Global Times*. Between 22 July and 1 October, China's National Day, the term "Hong Kong independence' circulated on social media, apparently with more than 10% directly reposted from *People's Daily* and *Global Times*, both of which are CCP controlled media.[30]

'The real transition in 1997 is not about sovereignty, it is about identity'

Perhaps we may get some insight from then Chief Secretary, Anson Chan who remarked in 1998: "The real transition (in 1997) is not about sovereignty, it is about identity." Mrs Chan said that for her, the defining moment occurred on the first national day celebration ceremony held in Hong Kong in the early morning of October 1 1997 with the raising of the flag and the playing of the national anthem of China.[31] She said she became emotional and felt she was Chinese. Between the lowering of one flag and the raising of another – in that instant when Hong Kong seemed truly without identity – identity became the issue, she reflected. She said[32]:

> That was one of the handover's defining moments and is the challenge Hong Kong faces today... As I watched the flag unfurl in the early morning breeze, I was suddenly filled with emotion... I think for the first time, I began to appreciate the spiritual propriety of Hong Kong's return to the mainland. I am Chinese.

Not all Hong Kong people feel the same. The issue of identifying with foreign countries, or colluding with a foreign agent (one of the main alleged criminal offences of Jimmy Lai, proprietor of *Apple Daily*) became controversial and dangerous after the imposition of the NSL in mid-2020. One of the awesome and unusual scenes during protests in 2019 was some protesters carrying the British or American flags, instead of waving the red flag of the PRC. They also would sing the British or American national anthem.

One of the protesters was called by the nickname "Captain America" because he dressed like the cartoon character. He has been prosecuted and jailed for nearly six years.[33] He is not alone. More than 10,000 people had been arrested on protest-related charges and almost 3,000 people charged by the end of December 2023, according to Hong Kong police.[34] Even Legco members and Tiananmen vigil organisers have been charged under the National Security Law. The first National Security Law trial involved Tong Ying-kit, a former waiter, who was found guilty of inciting secession and terrorism. He was sentenced to nine years in prison. Tong's crime was actually flying a flag with a forbidden slogan. He rode a motorbike into police officers while flying a flag with the protest slogan – "liberate Hong Kong, revolution of the times" which was advocated by the jailed localist activist Edward Leung.[35] Now let's go back and examine what happened a few years back which allowed the young activists to awaken and explode when the extradition bill provided a spark.

'Dissident youth' who strive to preserve a distinct local identity and values

Joshua Wong became a prominent public figure in 2012 as one of the leaders of a campaign by students – many of whom, including Wong himself, were still at school – against a government plan to impose a compulsory National Education subject on local schools. The government backed down and made the subject optional.[36] Joshua and his peer group had scored an early political success. Many of them were only 14 or 15 years old.[37]

One of their reasons for opposing the National Education subject was that it was to be taught in the Chinese national language, Putonghua, which is generally used everywhere in China as the official language; the written version is in simplified Chinese characters, rather than the traditional ones still widely used in Hong Kong. The secondary students defended their parents' Cantonese language, which is the usual language of instruction in local schools and became an official language in Hong Kong after a struggle by professional teachers back in the 1970s.

In 2014 Joshua led youngsters to occupy a "protest space" outside the government headquarters, which the government had decided to fence off. This led to the beginning of the Umbrella Revolution occupations. Finding the students already in possession of a large space in Central, Benny Tai, the legal professor-activist, announced the start of "love and peace demonstration in occupying Central" which he had been urging for months.[38]

The protesters occupied three spaces in Central, Causeway Bay, and Mong Kok for 79 days but failed to attract widespread public support. The two and a half months' occupation was peaceful, romantic, and involved enormous numbers of protestors and participants but reaped no immediate result. The government refused to compromise or negotiate. Finally, the movement burnt out, and the protesters withdrew from the occupied districts voluntarily.[39] This long struggle nurtured a generation of public-spirited young activists, ready to explode when triggered by the tabling of the extradition bill in March 2019.

In the wake of their sprouting local identity, youngsters started to lament the pan-democrats' way of handling political issues. The latter seemed to be satisfied with the continual postponement of universal suffrage, but they remained the biggest opposition party in the Hong Kong Legislative Council. The younger generation was more concerned with preserving a high degree of Hong Kong autonomy, the idea of separation from the ideology of socialist China, and preserving Hong Kong's unique way of life.

Some may go further to create a kind of Hong Kong ethnic group. Owen Chow was arrested and charged with a national security offence: joining a primary election. He told the court that he tried to tone down his election wording and leaflets after deciding to remain in the primary poll, changing his slogan from "say no to colonisation, ethnic group resists against tyranny" to "resist tyranny, defend our dignity." Chow also said he avoided wording that might be seen as "acute" or phrases that may be interpreted as breaching the security legislation.

Others, like Nathan Law, Ivan Lam and Agnes Chow, called for "self-determination." [40] One explanation came from an ordinary defendant in a riot court case. Defending himself, he said that

the government only sees people using violent means to forward their views, they don't see there is no channel, no peaceful way for people to assemble, to speak their opposition against government policy. And neither did the authorities listen. There was no democratic voice in the legislative council. Neither was there any public domain or avenue for people to voice out their resentment. Even if there was an outcry, the government was reluctant to take heed of it.[41]

For the first time in Hong Kong protest history, the protesters made it impossible to ignore them. As the mantra went, "if we burn, they burn with us" which denoted the protesters' heartfelt determination to change the political system.

Winnie Yu Wai-ming was a nurse and founder of a trade union for hospital workers, later one of the 47 people charged with national security offences over a primary election. Her interpretation of "mutual destruction" was to let "Hong Kong come first," to defend Hong Kong's interests by having universal suffrage in the Legislative Council and the election of the Chief Executive.[42]

For these activists, the main thing was to preserve and insist on Hong Kong's own culture, language, and values which were separate from the ideology, values, language, and culture of China. In a courtroom statement, Yu reflected on the role that medics played during the 2019 protests and unrest, as well as a general strike held by the Hospital Authority union in February 2020 urging the government to fully shut its borders with mainland China due to COVID-19. She defended putting a stop to the "compromise and criticise" tactic that pan-democrats had advocated. The phrase "compromise and criticise" was coined by veteran moderate democrat Frederick Fung, who promoted a mild approach when negotiating with the authorities. "The meaning is… in the past, pan-democrats lacked willpower when negotiating with the government. They were prone to making concessions," Yu said.

She added that she believed the legislature should be made up of lawmakers with stronger willpower who would hold the government accountable and fight for the five demands popularised during the anti-extradition protests. She said that the government was refusing to listen to the public's views and using violence to oppress people. People then used violence to respond to this violent oppression. She said there should be a "breakthrough," there must be systemic reform, or even "completely turning over the system and starting anew."[43]

These young activists and their supporters wanted to preserve the distinct identity of Hong Kong culture and Hong Kong people as a unique community different from mainland China, calling for a breakthrough and starting a new system. Owen Chow, another of the 47, told a court hearing that he wished to defend Hong Kong's high degree of autonomy and Hong Kong people ruling Hong Kong, as stipulated in the Joint Declaration. He said this was different from advocating Hong Kong independence.[44]

Severing 'yellow economic circle' financial support to protesters

In late 2023, Hong Kong police arrested former Demosisto chairperson Ivan Lam and some other former young activists, apparently sending a warning to the "yellow economic circle" which was set up in the wake of the crackdown in 2019. Police officers raided the office of shopping platform Mee, an online app that lists some members of the "yellow economic circle," a network of businesses that supported the pro-democracy protests in 2019. The former Demosisto members launched the app after the movement died down in 2020 because of the pandemic and the promulgation of the National Security Law.[45]

Demosisto was a political party formed in 2016 with the aim of gaining autonomy and self-determination for Hong Kong, and in the same year it won a seat in Hong Kong's Legislative Council elections. Its founding members included prominent activists Joshua Wong, Agnes Chow and Nathan Law.

The "yellow economic circle," a bottom-up campaign of consumer activism, became a phenomenon during the 2019 protests, with several businesses donating profits to funds that supported protesters. However, it has been denounced as a kind of "soft resistance" by state-controlled newspapers. Over the years, the yellow economy has dwindled. Many small restaurants and retail stores have quietly removed protest-related decorations, redacted slogans once written on their walls, or taken down their Lennon walls. The future of the yellow economy seemed bleak. People in the yellow economy circle did not expect any pro-democracy businesses to launch any major campaigns.[46]

Demosisto disbanded on 30 June 2020, the same day Hong Kong's National Security Law came into force. Lam was sentenced to prison alongside Wong and Chow in December 2020 for their roles in the anti-government protests in 2019, but Lam was released in April 2021 after serving five months. Wong has been in prison ever since and is facing subversion charges under the National Security Law.

The idea of localism

The whole idea of localism, to a certain extent, sprouted from a book, "On the Hong Kong City State" by Dr. Horace Wan Chin and an analytical op-editorial feature by the Hong Kong University Students' Union (HKUSU) *Undergrad* magazine, which attracted criticism from Leung Chun-ying, then Chief Executive of the Hong Kong SAR government.[47]

In addition, the advocacy of Edward Leung, a mainland-born Hong Kong University student, helped to consolidate the ideology and spread it to other youngsters, who set up different kinds of party or organisation agitating for different degrees of autonomy, or independence, from the Central government.[48] Finding it unlikely to get democracy through street protests, they turned to elections, hoping to win a seat so they could continue their movement inside the legislative chamber. Edward Leung knew he was likely to be disqualified from joining the election, although he was ready to sign any pledges, such as swearing his loyalty to the Basic Law, the mini-constitution of Hong Kong. Sure enough, he was not allowed to run. He found replacements, and two friends ran in the election on his behalf, and were duly elected.

Though appearing briefly in the Hong Kong Legislative Council, the replacements were both disqualified, allegedly for not properly swearing their loyalty to the authorities. As Baggio Leung Chung-hang, one of the young elected legislators who is now self-exiled because of activism, vividly put it: apparently they were walking on the water, throwing a pile of floating devices; when they threw the last one, they had to jump into the ocean and drowned.[49]

One of the powerful slogans created by Edward Leung and his peer group – "Liberate (or reclaim) Hong Kong, revolution of our times" – was heard on the streets all through the anti-extradition movement in 2019. As the saying went, "to reclaim Hong Kong" meant "to reclaim the liberty enjoyed in Hong Kong during the century of British colonial rule and in particular in the last three decades."[50]

Though both Edward Leung and Joshua Wong were behind bars in 2019, Edward Leung did write a letter urging the protesters to stick to peaceful means and not engage in any violent endeavours, which might have serious consequences.[51] In fact, when the Hong Kong government complained that they could not talk to a leaderless movement, one of the main reasons why it was leaderless was because key figures had been jailed. Leung has since been released at the end of a six-year jail term for "rioting" during the 2016 unrest in Mong Kok. Even though he has served his sentence and was released in early January 2022, he remains under a "supervision order" requiring him to delete his social media account and not talk to the media. "I must keep a low profile and deactivate my social media accounts," he wrote.[52]

"Liberate Hong Kong, revolution of our times" has since the imposition of the National Security Law become taboo. Any possessor of the slogan, whether it is shown in public or just stored in a tote bag or at home, risks being persecuted. A documentary entitled "Revolution of the Times" was barred from screens in Hong Kong, as was the documentary "Inside the Red Brick Wall" which depicted what happened when the Hong Kong Polytechnic University was besieged by police. [53]

Difference between newspaper tycoon and young dissident

According to evidence in Jimmy Lai's NSL and sedition case, Joshua Wong rejected Lai's idea of "one Hong Kong person, one letter," writing to the American President Trump to lobby him to put sanctions on China and the HKSAR government. Wong thought that Hong Kong democracy should be fought for by Hong Kong people and not by American people.[54] US politicians gave high praise to Joshua Wong and pledged to defend Hong Kong's freedom. But when China cracked down, Wong found himself with nowhere to go. He tried to reach out via his close allies in the US, wanting to hide in the US Consulate General in Hong Kong while waiting for asylum in America. Unfortunately that did not materialise.[55]

During that time, the defunct *Apple Daily* reportedly said that four activists had unsuccessfully attempted to take refuge in the US Consulate General in Hong Kong.[56] The media did not expose the names of the activists until 2023. Wong was the face of the protest, who was very well connected globally and in particular personally linked to heavyweight politicians such as Nancy Pelosi. But even so, that didn't get him anywhere when he was desperately in need of help.

The US feared, perhaps, that if the US Consulate General in Hong Kong was to shelter Joshua, it would be seen as a hostile move and might invite retaliation such as kidnapping Americans or other Chinese. After the consideration of national interest and personal interest, the US national interest prevailed.[57] This could, of course also be said of British policy in Hong Kong over the years: At the end of the day, the national interest overrides any local consideration.[58] The difference was that the US government and President Trump had been voicing support for Hong Kong democracy, which gave the protesters enormous encouragement, reflected in the waving of American flags. Hong Kong protesters felt they had solid backing from America. There was bipartisan support in US political circles for local democratic groups, in particular personal meetings with young activists such as Joshua Wong, Nathan Law, media proprietor Jimmy Lai, and Canto-pop singer Denise Ho. They thought they had the backing of the most powerful nation in the world.[59] But that turned into a false hope. Wong has, since the imposition of the NSL, been detained on various criminal charges, including the serious matter of colluding with foreign agents.[60]

Activists and the prison system

The arrival in Hong Kong prisons of a large number of articulate and educated youngsters presented an uncomfortable challenge for the Correctional Services Department, which runs the local prison system.

Owen Chow incurred a series of penalties, including an additional day in jail and solitary confinement for unauthorised possession of an egg tart. Clearly the Correctional Services were unhappy with his frequent communications to the outside of information about life behind bars. For instance, an art book was banned because of a nude picture: Botticelli's *Venus*. He told the outside world of the ignorance and embarrassing lack of knowledge of the Correctional Services. He and one of his lawyers were also charged because of his passing on a complaint letter to the lawyer to complain to the Ombudsman of his maltreatment by the Correctional Services.[61]

Tonyee Chow, a barrister jailed over June 4 commemorations, was repeatedly kept in solitary confinement for receiving too many letters. She was deprived of books, which she treasured most, and watching TV or listening to radio broadcasts. She was also deprived of the usual hour's free time in the open air, a chance to enjoy the sun. Still, she urged friends and supporters on her Facebook page not to be deterred from writing to her.[62]

Among these young activists, there was one common thing: that they did not want the authorities to bend the rules in their favour. They would not submit to restrictions in order to get bail. For instance, Gwyneth Ho and Tonyee Chow both refused bail because it would have required them not to talk to the media and not to access social media. As a result, they were detained without bail for more than two years, waiting for a trial date.[63]

From Hong Kong Chinese to 'Hongkonger': From 1989 to 2019

Why was there such a big divide of views towards the sovereign between the older generation and the younger generation? Because of the false hope which One Country, Two Systems gave to Hong Kong people, leading to the understanding of the younger generation that they would have a very different system from China. The originator of One Country Two Systems, Chinese leader Deng Xiaoping, probably thought China would move closer to the Hong Kong system after the mid-1980s, when the Chinese government signed the Joint Declaration. He would never have imagined that after almost 40 years, the CCP ruling mainland China would have abandoned his vision and had forced draconian mainland-style laws upon Hong Kong.

When Hong Kong reverted to Chinese sovereignty in 1997, expectations were high both in Beijing and among the pro-Beijing stakeholders in Hong Kong. They believed that identification with the Chinese nation would grow among the local population, particularly the younger generations, which would eventually lead to Hong Kong's full integration into China. However, in 2012, it was precisely the youngsters, the ones educated after the handover, who were most critical of the mainland. A June 2013 poll showed that identification with Hong Kong had even increased since the handover, with 62% of the population identifying primarily with Hong Kong and 38% with Hong Kong exclusively. More surprisingly, the primary proportion was 84.3% among the 18–29 group, of whom 55.8% identified exclusively with Hong Kong. That was one year after teenage activists had successfully protested against the government's national and moral education schemes.[64]

A media proprietor made his voice heard

Besides young dissenters, there was Jimmy Lai and his using *Apple Daily* as a platform to promote democratic ideas, to resolve the differences between the radicals and the compromising pan-democrats, to advocate and connect with overseas politicians and columnists. For instance, he used his own column, "Sink or Swim, Smile", to promote the values and his vision; he used the op-ed page to carry overseas columnists' points of view; he was actively involved in setting up editorial policy, under which the publisher Cheung Kim-hung, and associate publisher Chan Pui-man were instructed to implement his vision. In addition, he recruited former leading editorial writer Fung Wai-kong to run an English version, which allowed more English-reading foreigners, especially American politicians and ordinary Americans to be informed of Hong Kong's situation, who in turn might support lobbying for foreign sanctions on the CCP and senior Hong Kong officials.[65]

The role of the media

Hong Kong people's expectations for their future were irreparably changed in 1989 when they saw the Tiananmen crackdown live on TV news and copiously covered in newspapers. For the first time, many had mixed feelings about what it meant to be Chinese.

Among them was Jimmy Lai, then a successful businessman in the clothing line. In a later interview, he said he didn't have much feeling for China until 1989 when he saw what happened to Beijing students. All of a sudden, he had a deep feeling for them. He described it as "amid absolute darkness, there was an apparent call from the mother."[66] He said he needed to make a difficult choice — leaving Hong Kong, a place where he had become rich through liberty and the free-market economy, or staying in this decadent city and continuing to contribute to civil society.

Indeed, what happened in mid 1989 triggered an unprecedented emigration from Hong Kong to Western countries. This mass departure included a large outflow of professionals. But Jimmy Lai saw an opportunity to join the media industry and started a brand new magazine, *Next*, after 1989 and the *Apple Daily*, a popular tabloid newspaper, in 1995. In 2003 more than half a million Hong Kong people took to the streets to protest against a proposed national security bill, which was later postponed indefinitely. This was the first major demonstration over a local issue to attract such a big crowd. *Apple Daily* played a part in mobilising people to take to the streets. For instance, they printed free posters with an A3 size mugshot of Tung Chee-hwa, the then Chief Executive of the Hong Kong SAR government, with a cake smashed in his face.

This was what commentators called "one daily newspaper, one magazine and two microphones" – referring to *Apple Daily*, *Next Magazine*, and *Commercial Radio's* morning and evening programmes – which moved hundreds and thousands of Hong Kong people from all walks of life, including bankers, legislators, professionals and priests, to share and express their resentment. *Apple Daily* continued its support for the democratic movement up to and through 2019. Lai used the Chinese print version to promote content which would support and arouse sympathy for protesters and their mission, also to advocate and mobilise people. The paper printed a free poster for protesters to be distributed by the Democratic Party during mass demonstrations.[67] The protest story was assigned prominence on the front page and as headline news so as to mobilise ordinary citizens to take to the streets.[68]

A former executive of *Apple Daily* gave evidence in Jimmy Lai's national security trial that he hoped to call for sanctions from the United States through a letter campaign to then American leader Donald Trump ahead of the national security law's enactment in 2020. An accomplice witness, the former publisher of *Apple Daily*, Cheung Kim-hung, recalled Lai instructing him to roll out the campaign, "One Hongkonger One Letter to Save Hong Kong," in May 2020. The daily published the campaign on its front page, appealing to people to participate and write to Trump with the letter, entitled "Mr President, please help us."

Lai also launched a new English digital version of *Apple Daily*, to include the voices of prominent overseas columnists, including then-US vice-president Mike Pence.[69] *Apple Daily* columnist Fung Hei-kin had suggested introducing the English edition to "break the monopoly" of the *South China Morning Post* in English newspapers. Lai stressed that readers would subscribe to *Apple Daily's* English version if it was "very different" from the *South China Morning Post*. Lai's own column, "Sink or Swim, Smile," continued to appear even after his first court appearance; he only stopped writing when actually charged with a criminal offence. [70] *Apple Daily* newspaper ran a front-page advertisement in May 2020 that said "freedom has become a crime". Just a year later it was raided by police, funds frozen and forced to close.

Apart from the *Apple Daily*, *Stand News* was the next to be targeted with by the authorities. The reason was that *Stand News* had been influential in 2019; on some important days such as 21 July and 1 July, the digital news site attracted more viewers than the *Apple Daily*.[71] However, no one knew when, how, or on what pretext the day of reckoning would arrive.

Chung Pui-kuen, former chief editor and founder of *Stand News*, apparently did not think there was any urgency to consider if they would be forced to shut down. However when *Apple Daily* was raided by 500 police officers, Chung started to take precautions, such as taking down old op-ed articles from the *Stand News* website.[72] Also, he started to make his staff redundant and then re-employ them at their suggestion, so they could collect long-service payments. He shifted the staff's monthly payday to the first day of the month to make sure they got paid if anything terrible happened. He knew it would come, but didn't know when and how. All he could do was to try to protect his colleagues as far as possible.

One risk was avoided by having a collective ownership. There would be no top-down instruction to change their stance, or to shut down as happened to *House News*. The boss, Choi Tung-ho disappeared for several weeks, then shut down *House News* when he returned to Hong Kong, without consulting the top editorial staff. It was later found out that Choi had been under house arrest in China. Both his personal and business security were threatened.[73]

Time ran out for *Stand News* at the end of December 2021. Directors and senior staff were arrested, 200 police raided the office and its accounts were frozen. Legal fall-out continues.

Collapse of civil society

The closure of newspapers was only part of a general assault on any part of civil society not controlled by or beholden to the government. In less than two years' after the imposition of the National Security Law, more than 60 non-government organisations were forced to shut or voluntarily closed themselves. Some, for instance Amnesty International Hong Kong, chose to move their offices elsewhere.[74] This was not an option available to local institutions, many of them not formed with official approval or commercial motives, but instead grown slowly over decades, and not without a lot of obstacles and challenges from the ruling colonial government. Some of them had been pioneers in early struggles for fairness and freedom under colonial rule, like the Professional Teachers Union, which campaigned successfully in the 70s for the use of Chinese in schools, the rights of certified teachers to equal pay, and other educational and social issues. A civil society painfully constructed over 100 years was destroyed in a matter of months.

NGOs under pressure: The Foreign Correspondents Club

The Foreign Correspondents Club (FCC), Hong Kong has a long history. It moved to Hong Kong from Shanghai in 1949. It occupied a variety of premises in the ensuing years, achieving legendary status with mentions in novels and films. In 1982 the Hong Kong Government offered it a new home in the northern part of the Dairy Farm building, one of the few historic buildings surviving in central Hong Kong. The other half of the building was offered to an arts group.

In 2018 the FCC discovered where the new "red line" was. The club was accustomed to inviting speakers of many persuasions to perform at lunch meetings. Previous visitors had included Chief Executives and other respectable figures. The club strayed into a minefield when it invited young activist Andy Chan Hao-Tian, head of the Hong Kong National Party, a tiny group with a handful of members, most of whom preferred to remain anonymous. Nevertheless, he was invited to speak on his vision of Hong Kong independence over lunch. The proceedings were moderated by Victor Mallet, a

Financial Times correspondent and the vice president of the club. The president was away on a work trip.

Before the meeting the club was urged to cancel it by the local office of China's Ministry of Foreign Affairs; they went ahead on the grounds that it was their function to provide journalists with exposure to a wide variety of political views, whether conservative or radical. On the day of the talk the police cordoned off the pavement outside the club, separating a dozen pro-Beijing protesters from arriving guests. Afterwards, the Ministry of Foreign Affairs in Hong Kong issued a strongly worded statement criticising the FCC for promoting Hong Kong independence and secession from the motherland by providing a platform for a separatist to spread his seditious idea of secession from mainland China.[75]

The unlucky Mr Mallet, as the moderator of the talk, was the first to be penalised. When his work visa expired later that year, it was not renewed. The *Financial Times* had to post him elsewhere. After his departure, he tried to re-enter Hong Kong, where he had lived for several years, to collect his belongings and help his family to relocate to his new post, but he was refused entry to the city.[76] The ban was an alarming signal to foreign correspondents. Both before and after the handover non-Chinese could either enter Hong Kong freely as tourists without a visa, or apply for a work visa if they had been offered work in Hong Kong. Mallet attempted to appeal to the Immigration Department but in vain. He could not re-enter Hong Kong even as a visitor.

After that, the Foreign Correspondents Club reviewed and amended its policy over press freedom issues. For instance, the annually organised Human Rights Press Awards were axed when it was noticed that the award list included several awards granted to the defunct digital *Stand News*.[77] The HRPA would have celebrated its 26th anniversary. It was set up by the FCC, Hong Kong Journalists Association and Amnesty International Hong Kong in 1996. In the light of the National Security Law indirectly forcing NGOs and other civil society organisations to shut down, Amnesty had moved out of Hong Kong; the HKJA had also opted out as an organiser from the HRPA but still participated.

Subsequent to the sudden cancellation by the president and board members, several members of the Press Freedom Committee and a board member resigned and quit the Club as a protest at the handling of the matter. One of the veteran correspondents, James Pomfret, disagreed with the then president who remarked that "journalists had to self-censor themselves" in Hong Kong.[78] It was a peculiar move to cancel the HRPA at the last moment. But the FCC reasoned that it had to protect its 100-strong staff and to maintain the well-being of the club. The club's premises are leased, not owned, so it stays at the pleasure of the government. At the time of the Human Rights Press Awards row it was awaiting renewal. The eventual renewed lease included a new term requiring the club "to safeguard national security and to sufficiently protect the Government's rights and interests."

The club was criticised by correspondent members and journalists for forfeiting the precious right of press freedom on the 40th anniversary of their move in 1982. Since then, the FCC board of governors decided that they will not issue any statement regarding press freedom issues such as journalists being arrested, detained, or charged unless they sought prior consent or consultation with the Hong Kong SAR government.[79] According to a source who was familiar with the situation, the president said "he had saved the club" by axing the HRPA, mainly because they had been awaiting a response from the SAR government regarding their lease. The lease to remain on the same heritage site was finally renewed in early 2023 for another three years – which was less than half of the previous usual lease duration of seven years.

Then president Keith Richberg stepped down as president and left Hong Kong in 2023 for Princeton University. He was succeeded by an editor of *Tatler* magazine, a lifestyle magazine. No correspondent wanted the job. In the new president's statement to members, he said he would prefer the club to take up issues concerning journalists and correspondents and not just act as a food and beverage club. This recognised the fundamental problem: the club in effect has a thriving business catering for "associate" (non-journalist) members who have no vote but pay much higher membership fees. This allows it to offer stellar services to correspondents but also makes it vulnerable to pressure. One local newspaper reported the lease renewal under the headline "FCC can stay – if it behaves." Members awaited further developments with some anxiety.[80]

In 2023, a variety of foreign correspondents, academics, and photographers were barred from entering Hong Kong without reasons being given. They are apparently regarded as not being friendly with Hong Kong, or even worse, as posing a threat to Hong Kong national security. These people included an award-winning Japanese photographer who had documented Hong Kong's social movement in 2019, turned it into a book, and held exhibitions in Japan. Foreign correspondents who had written about Hong Kong, including a freelance Japanese journalist and a Western correspondent, were also refused access to Hong Kong. Apparently, the red line the journalists had trodden on was writing about the social movement in 2019. An academic who used to teach at the Chinese University of Hong Kong was refused renewal of her work visa and subsequently fired by the university. She had been conducting research and writing on the 1989 Beijing Tiananmen movement crackdown.[81]

NGOs under pressure: The Hong Kong Journalists Association (HKJA)

The HKJA is a long-standing union which helps to provide solidarity and help to rank and file journalists when they meet with obstacles and arrest at work.[82] It was founded in 1968 after an incident in which firefighters turned their hoses on journalists who were monitoring their work. A non-profit organisation dedicated to defending press freedom in Hong Kong, the HKJA stands as one of the last organisations advocating on behalf of journalists in the territory, following a government crackdown that has gutted civil society since the enactment of the National Security Law in 2020. Over the past decade, the organisation has worked independently to support journalists despite escalating harassment from the authorities.

During the 2019 social movement, the relationship between the union and the authorities became strained, in particular when journalists and photographers were under attack by tear gas, water cannons, bean bag bullets, rubber bullets, and other weapons used by the police.[83] Meanwhile the authorities complained about bias among journalists, young journalists without proper identification, underage supposed reporters, fake journalists and, of course, coverage they did not like.

Many journalists and photographers were injured; most seriously an Indonesian female reporter who was shot in the eye during a live broadcast in Wan Chai.[84] In the middle of confrontations between the police and protesters, journalists came under pressure and sometimes were used by both sides as a buffer while trying to do their job. Many journalists were injured and some were harassed by the police, including Ronson Chan, who was seen to be shot in the face with teargas to his face, and also had his ID card shown on a live broadcast by police who asked him to show his identity.[85] Chan was later sentenced to five days' imprisonment for obstructing police in 2023.

The HKJA appealed to the public, who reacted promptly to donate money for a "protect journalists fund" which in 2023 still maintained slightly more than HK$2 million. The fund has since helped a journalist hospitalised with an eye injury and another journalist with the expenses of an appeal from a conviction, after he was beaten up and then prosecuted during his reporting on the street in 2014.[86]

In late 2023, the HKJA was shortlisted for an award by Reporters Sans Frontières. They said the HKJA, a non-profit-making organisation, was among the last remaining NGOs striving to protect journalists' interests after the imposition of the National Security Law.[87] It had survived when other civil society institutions had either moved their base out of Hong Kong (e.g., Amnesty International) or disbanded themselves altogether (e.g., the Professional Teacher Union, Hong Kong Federation of Unions, and the Hong Kong Alliance in Support of Patriotic Democratic Movements of China).[88]

In fact, in early 2022, the association was under tremendous pressure to disband after *Apple Daily* and *Stand News* had shut down in 2021, and *Citizen News* voluntarily closed its doors in early 2022. In an Emergency General Meeting, the union decided to lower the requirement to disband the union from the consent of two-thirds of full members to just one half of full members' consent.[89] There was another challenge in that many journalists had lost their jobs or decided to leave Hong Kong. There was a serious lack of members to stand and be elected as executive committee members. Worse still, for three consecutive years after 2021, the union was unable to hold any fund-raising dinners, its main means of financial support, as no hotel would dare to rent a room out for an HKJA event.

Also, the chairperson, Ronson Chan, was under arrest and charged with obstructing police, which in fact was because he refused to show his ID card when accosted by a plainclothes policeman who showed no police credential. He was convicted and sentenced to five days in jail. The judge said the offence was so serious that she could not give a lighter penalty such as a fine or social service, which are usually the usual penalty for this kind of offence. Chan applied for an appeal on 25 September 2023 and was given bail on condition of reporting to the police twice a week. In late February 2024, the outcome of his appeal is still pending. [90]

Compared with the FCC the union did have one important advantage. The government was not its landlord. When the FCC moved to its present site in the early 1980s the British Hong Kong administration granted the heritage premises in Ice House Street for the use of both press clubs. However, as the HKJA could not afford to share the renovation expenses, they were put in a tiny room in the basement. After a year or so, HKJA decided to move out and find its own office in Wan Chai. Although this was before the handover, given the changing political environment the HKJA Executive Committee envisaged that they might have problems in the future if they rented an office. So with help from members and the like, they raised enough money to buy an office by selling "bricks" to members and other well-wishers.

However, efforts to persuade the union to disband itself continued. The use of tax evasion or financial fraud charges as an excuse to crackdown on dissidents is commonly found in China. In Hong Kong it was unheard of until recently, when the abuse of government powers has become commonplace. A pro-democracy café, for example, reported visits every week from "various government departments" including the Food and Environmental Hygene Department, the Fire Services Department, the Agriculture, Fisheries and Conservation Department, the Inland Revenue Department, the Hong Kong Police Force, the Labour Department and the Buildings Department. The owners eventually took the hint and closed. [91]

In January 2024, the Inland Revenue Department issued a letter to the HKJA demanding HK$400,000 in outstanding tax for 2018–19. It further sought details of the union's annual revenue from 2018 to 2024. All the chairpersons and executive committee members who had held office in those six years also received the letter. This looked like the beginning of the end. To many, it was seen as a repressive measure to combat the HKJA, which is the leading trade union of journalists across the political spectrum. [92] One former chairperson was terrified to have heard this news, and wrote an email to the incumbent chairperson and all executive members, saying that HKJA should check if the tax bureau also reviewed other press organisations, namely the pro-establishment Hong Kong News Executives' Association and the pro-Beijing Hong Kong Federation of Hong Kong journalists. If not, this should be regarded as discrimination.[93]

Digital media

The history of Hong Kong's protest movement provides a test of the theory that the rise of digital media has changed the political landscape. Social media use enhanced media's influence in the social movement of the 21st century and in particular in 2014, which in turn helped to sprout digital media further, professional and amateur, in colleges, secondary schools, and even primary schools.

In the post-2014 era, one of the interesting features in the media industry was the sprouting of digital news media. The advantage of setting up small scale digital media was that they had low running costs and did not require a big investment. Also the operation of news coverage could be flexible, independent and allow freedom for rank and file journalists to pick up issues of their own interest. The influence of each news outlet would be relatively smaller, which meant they would not attract attention or any subsequent intervention from the authorities. Hong Kong people are wired and digitally literate. The territory has more mobile phones than people. They would naturally take up the habit of reading online news. It is easier and cheaper to start up a new media by using online resources and online operation, and particularly attractive if the target audience is the younger generation.

How to resist "political pressure" and market factors were the main concerns of the small scale "we-media" and online news websites. Those who were critical constantly faced direct and indirect interference and influence from the government, political parties, politicians, and other stakeholders. They were also affected by cash flow threats such as boycotts from advertisers. In order to maintain an independent editorial policy, the new media companies had to avoid relying on official tolerance or advertising revenue, addictions which would harm institutional and organisational independence. Most of them, in the end, relied mainly on financial support from their readers.

After the failure of the Umbrella Movement, there was a blossoming of independent digital media on the news scene. For instance, the defunct *House News* re-launched as the leading pro-democracy free digital news, *Stand News,* after missing covering the whole Umbrella Movement. *House News* was set up in 2012 during the anti-Moral and National Education movement. In the summer of 2014, before the Umbrella Movement actually started, the *House News'* proprietor Tony Tsoi announced that the outlet would close without giving any explanation. He was later reported to have said that prior to that decision, he was under house arrest in China. He was threatened that his business in China would be affected, as well as his own safety.[94]

When *Stand News* was to be launched, with the same group of senior management and many former journalists who used to work for the ill-fated *House News*, the former chief editor of *House News* and founder of the new site, Chung Pui-kuen, restructured the whole set-up with five directors, so that *Stand News* would not be easily shut down by just one proprietor. He hoped that would allow *Stand News* to have a long life, if not a permanent life in Hong Kong's unstable political environment. However, even with this thoughtful arrangement, *Stand News* was forced to shut down on 29 December 2021 after 200 police raided the office, the two chief editors were arrested on sedition charges and their office bank account was frozen.

InmediaHK (formerly Hong Kong In-media) was a pioneer of digital media which used to cover social issues, in particular the urbanisation of land, and other controversies like the demolition of the old Star Ferry Pier, the Queen's Pier and so on. In 2023, they celebrated their 19th anniversary,which meant they had been set up early enough to report on the campaign against the national security bill.[95] Apparently out of the concerns about political sensitivity, they quietly changed their Chinese name in 2020 to remove the word "independent".

Hong Kong Free Press is the only English daily news website, organised by a young Englishman after he graduated from the HKU media centre's MA programme in 2015. HKFP upholds a relatively independent editorial policy, focused on selected local news mainly related to politics, court news, and minority news.

Citizen News was another well-received digital news site focussing on political news, in particular court reports. It was set up by friends of Kevin Lau, former chief editor of the prestigious Chinese language newspaper *Ming Pao Daily News*, who was stabbed nearly to death by an attacker. Sadly, although the stabber was caught, the mastermind remains at large. *Citizen News* was founded with seed money donated by friends, lawyer friends, and supporters to try to track down the real culprit. It shut down in January 2022 immediately after the closure of *Stand News*, simply out of fear that it would be targeted next.

After the 2019 movement, and the swift passage of the National Security Law in mid-2020, major oppositional media such as *Apple Daily*, *Stand News*, and *Citizen News* were forced to shut down one after another. Almost 1,000 journalists lost their jobs. Some chose to change career while some left Hong Kong for good. Those who wished to stay and carry on with their journalistic work started to organise small-scale digital media with a handful of journalists with a similar vision. Others might just start a digital media on their own.

Journalism has become a stressful pursuit. Besides attempts at disinformation and framing of the movement as having a motive of pushing for "Hong

Kong independence," the use of intimidation tactics including surveillance, visible tailing, and personal threats via letters to the victim and family members is now routine. "White terror," imagined or otherwise, imposes stress on frontline journalists and editors. Journalists find themselves lying in bed wide awake at four or five in the early morning, because that's the hour police usually knock at the door and arrest journalists and activists. The hours were long and fearful for people like Tonyee Chow, the barrister-turned-activist, for Ronson Chan, the chairperson of Hong Kong Journalists Association, and Kwan Chun-hoi, who eventually closed his bookshop because every day he had someone downstairs watching him and his shop. Kwan did not sleep well. Many friends urged him to leave his premises and Hong Kong for good. So he closed the bookshop and took a break in Japan where his wife lived. He returned to Hong Kong after a year and continued his news website, *Hong Kong Features*.

What is left: Soft resistance?

Two decades after the return to Chinese rule, it was apparent that Hong Kong's identity had changed in a way unwelcome to its new rulers. Five years after the events of 2019, the Hong Kong government is still ultra-sensitive to any suggestion that local people are not devoted admirers of the mainland government. Even polite criticism is condemned as "soft resistance."

A good example is the continued legal squabble over the national anthem. If you Google "Hong Kong national anthem" you will usually be directed to the protest song "Glory to Hong Kong." This is an understandable error. Hong Kong does not have a national anthem; it uses the Chinese national anthem, "March of the Volunteers." At some sporting events the organisers played "Glory to Hong Kong" in error when a Hong Kong team had won. Some sportsmen and sportswomen and indeed some Hong Kong athletic organisations have been penalised for not being able to stop overseas sports organisers playing the song during medal ceremonies.[96] The Hong Kong SAR government has repeatedly asked Google to replace the song with the Chinese national anthem but Google refused. Its algorithm gives people what they want. So the authorities applied for an injunction banning the song. The Court of First Instance refused the injunction, saying there was already a law against offending the national anthem. The government successfully appealed.

The government also prosecuted an elderly busker who played the tune from "Glory to Hong Kong" on the Chinese musical instrument, the *erhu*, in public places. He was acquitted by a magistrate, but the authorities appealed until he was sentenced to jail for being a busker playing a forbidden tune. The incident was widely regarded as a ridiculous episode which showed the Hong

Kong and China governments as obsessed with national pride and worried about face. On the other hand, a well-received book with the title "I Don't Want to be Chinese Again" has been reprinted almost 50 times.[97]

Notes

1 Felicity Lewis, "Hong Kong People, Take Revenge": How Did Hong Kong Get Here?, *Sydney Morning Herald*, 19 November 2019, accessed at: https://www.smh.com.au/world/asia/hong-kong-people-take-revenge-how-did-hong-kong-get-here-20191118-p53bob.html; Kris Cheng, Explainer: Hong Kong's Five Demands – Amnesty for All Arrested Protesters, *Hong Kong Free Press*, 13 April 2020, accessed at: https://hongkongfp.com/2019/12/25/explainer-hong-kongs-five-demands-amnesty-arrested-protesters/

2 Francis L. F. Lee, Samson Yuen, Gary Tang, and Edmund W. Cheng, Hong Kong's Summer of Uprising, *China Review*, 19(4) , 1–32, 2019 Chinese University of Hong Kong Press.

3 Si Liao, to settle privately without reporting to the police or to the judiciary; Emma Graham-Harrison, Lily Kuo and Guardian Reporter in Hong Kong, A Battle For The Soul of the City: Why Violence Has Spiralled in the Hong Kong Protests, *The Guardian*, 6 October 2019, accessed at: https://www.theguardian.com/world/2019/oct/06/a-battle-for-the-soul-of-the-city-why-violence-has-spiralled-in-the-hong-kong-protests

4 Frank Reichert, Adelaide Tsz Nok Au, Anna Julia Fiedler, How Collective Demands Strengthen Sympathy for Normative and Non-Normative Protest Action: The Example of Hong Kong's Anti-Extradition Law Amendment Bill Protests, *Sociology Compass*, 30 October 2023, accessed at: https://doi.org/10.1111/soc4.13169

5 Weiboscope HKU, Beijing Constructs an "Independence" Plot for Hong Kong Protests through Information Operations, *Global Voices*, 1 November 2019, accessed at: https://globalvoices.org/2019/11/01/beijing-constructs-an-independence-plot-for-hong-kong-protests-through-information-operations/

6 A BNO passport holder could use it as a travel document outside Hong Kong. There was no right of abode in the UK.

7 The special "5 + 1" plan is to allow BNO Hong Kong passport holders to apply for permanent residence after the 2019 crackdown.

8 Cheryl Tung, UK Relaxes Partner Rules for Its BNO Visa Scheme for Hong Kongers, *RFA Cantonese*, 2 February 2024, accessed at: https://www.rfa.org/english/news/china/china-hong-kong-bno-visas-02022024153721.html. "Liberate Hong Kong, Revolution of the Times." The clarion call of the current wave of ongoing protests – also often translated as "liberate" or "reclaim" – traces its roots back to the election campaign of activist Edward Leung, currently serving a six-year prison sentence for rioting and assaulting a police officer during the so-called Fishball Revolution of 2016. See Mary Hui, A Guide to the Most Important Chants of Hong Kong's Protests Rallying Cries, *Quartz*, 2 September 2019, accessed at: https://qz.com/1699119/chants-and-slogans-of-hong-kongs-protests-explained

9 Irene Chan, Hong Kong Nat. Security Police Charge Man over Wearing Alleged "Seditious" Shirt at Airport, *Hong Kong Free Press*, 29 November 2023, accessed at: https://hongkongfp.com/2023/11/29/hong-kong-national-security-police-charge-man-over-wearing-alleged-seditious-shirt-at-airport/

10 The documentaries: *Inside the Red Brick Wall* and *Revolution of Our Times* documented the confrontations on the campuses of the Chinese University of Hong Kong and the Hong Kong Polytechnic University. Neither of these films can be

screened in Hong Kong. Hong Kong Film Group Cancels Public Screening of Protest Documentary, *RFA*, 15 March 2021, accessed at: https://www.rfa.org/english/news/china/film-03152021124457.html

11 Figo Chan ho-wun did reflect on 2019 protest strategies. He thought if they did otherwise, the effect (of suppression) may not be so strong. 難抗命續發聲　陳皓桓：人在希望在　籲公民社會思反修例運動失敗 「不承認怎面對未來」, accessed at: https://news.mingpao.com/pns/港聞/article/20221114/s00002/1668364263288/難抗命續發聲-陳皓桓-人在希望在-籲公民社會思反修例運動失敗-「不承認怎面對未來」

12 Kris Cheng, Hongkongers Identifying as "Chinese" at Record Low; Under 10% of Youth "Proud" to Be Citizens – Poll, *Hong Kong Free Press*, 28 June 2019, accessed at: https://hongkongfp.com/2019/06/28/hongkongers-identifying-chinese-record-low-10-youth-proud-citizens-poll/; PORI later announced that they will not be able continue their surveys of Hong Kong people's identity and their sentiment towards mainland China because of political pressure. Mandy Cheng, Hong Kong Pollster to Stop Publicly Releasing Results of Surveys on 10 Topics, No Questions on China Human Rights, *Hong Kong Free Press*, 28 July 2023, accessed at: https://hongkongfp.com/2023/07/28/hong-kong-pollster-to-stop-publicly-releasing-results-of-surveys-on-10-topics-no-questions-on-china-human-rights/

13 Mandy Cheng, Hong Kong Pollster to Stop Publicly Releasing Results of Surveys on 10 Topics, No Questions on China Human Rights, *Hong Kong Free Press*, 28 July 2023, accessed at: https://hongkongfp.com/2023/07/28/hong-kong-pollster-to-stop-publicly-releasing-results-of-surveys-on-10-topics-no-questions-on-china-human-rights/

14 In the survey, 53% of the interviewees identified as Hongkongers, while 11% identified as Chinese. Additionally, 12% identified as "Chinese in Hong Kong," and 23% identified themselves as "Hongkongers in China." Ibid.

15 Kris Cheng, Hongkongers Identifying as "Chinese" at Record Low; Under 10% of Youth "Proud" to Be Citizens – Poll, *Hong Kong Free Press*, 31 March 2020, accessed at: https://hongkongfp.com/2019/06/28/hongkongers-identifying-chinese-record-low-10-youth-proud-citizens-poll/

16 Peter Lee, Highest Number of Hong Kong Adults Identify as "Chinese" since 2018, Survey Finds, *Hong Kong Free Press*, 22 June 2022, accessed at: https://hongkongfp.com/2022/06/22/highest-number-of-hong-kong-adults-identify-as-chinese-since-2018-survey-finds/

17 Ibid.

18 Be water, my friend – martial arts master Bruce Lee's motto. He said, "Be like water; water has form and yet it has no form. It is the softest element on earth, yet it penetrates the hardest rock. It has no shape of its own, yet it can take any shape in which it is placed." Bruce Lee, *Striking thoughts: Bruce Lee's Wisdom for Daily Living*, Tokyo: Tuttle Publishing, 2000, 108.

19 Silvia Frosina, Digital Revolution: How Social Media Shaped the 2019 Hong Kong Protests Two Years On, *ISPI*, 8 June 2021, accessed at: https://www.ispionline.it/en/publication/digital-revolution-how-social-media-shaped-2019-hong-kong-protests-30756

20 Natasha Khan and Wenxin Fan "Prepared to Die": Hong Kong Protesters Embrace Hard-Core Tactics, Challenge Beijing, *Wall Street Journal*, 6 August 2019, accessed at: https://www.wsj.com/articles/prepared-to-die-hong-kong-protesters-embrace-hard-core-tactics-challenge-beijing-11565038264

21 Shibani Mahtani and Tiffany Liang, Thousands Link Hands in a Hong Kong Vigil Protesting a More Aggressive Beijing, *The Washington Post*, 23 August 2019, accessed at: https://www.washingtonpost.com/world/asia_pacific/thousands-link

-hands-in-a-hong-kong-vigil-protesting-a-more-aggressive-beijing/2019/08/23/
dc1656a0-c55b-11e9-8bf7-cde2d9e09055_story.html

22 Political Crisis in Hong Kong, *RFA*, 20 November 2019, accessed at: https://www
.rfa.org/english/news/special/hongkong-protest/

23 Weiboscope HKU, Beijing Constructs an "Independence" Plot for Hong Kong
Protests through Information Operations, *Global Voices*, 1 November 2019,
updated 31 March 2020, accessed at: https://hongkongfp.com/2019/11/05/beijing
-constructs-independence-plot-hong-kong-protests-information-operations/

24 Ibid.

25 For example, a Hong Kong actor and an ex-cop, Wong Hei, who sympathised with
the protesters, was labelled a "pro-Hong Kong independence" actor by Chinese
social media entertainment news outlets and celebrity fan communities. Hong
Kong students' class boycotts were labelled "pro-Hong Kong independence" acts
on both official and commercial social media public accounts.

26 Li was the most unexpected victim of such political labelling. On Chinese social
media, including Weibo and WeChat, he was accused of sponsoring the protests
by a number of pro-Beijing online opinion leaders and HK-related Chinese social
media news outlets. *supra* note 23.

27 On 20 August 2019, a female journalist was stabbed in the stomach at a Lennon
Wall in Tseung Kwan O. She was left in critical condition. On 29 October, a teenage boy was stabbed by a mainland Chinese tourist at a Tai Po Lennon Wall. The
attacker reportedly took down pro-democracy posters on the wall and shouted
"Hong Kong is part of China" before he attacked his victim, who was handing out
flyers. Holmes Chan, 26-Year-Old Woman in Critical Condition after Knife Attack
at Hong Kong "Lennon Wall," *Hong Kong Free Press*, 20 August 2019, accessed
at: https://hongkongfp.com/2019/08/20/26-year-old-hong-kong-woman-critical
-condition-knife-attack-lennon-wall-tseung-kwan-o/

28 *Supra* note 23.

29 Ibid. Thereafter the frequencies of three key terms related to Hong Kong protests
surged: Hong Kong independence; Demands; Fugitive.

30 Beijing Constructs an "Independence" Plot for Hong Kong Protests through
Information Operations, *Global Voices*, 5 November 2019, updated 31 March 2020,
accessed at: https://hongkongfp.com/2019/11/05/beijing-constructs-independence
-plot-hong-kong-protests-information-operations/

31 The Hong Konger: Jimmy Lai's Extraordinary Struggle for Freedom, Acton
Institute, film premiered on 19 April 2023, accessed at: https://www.youtube.com/
watch?v=NwwxNDP2Fss&t=524s

32 Anson Chan speech at the annual dinner of the Asia Society, in Washington DC, 11
June 1998. Accessed at· https://www.info.gov.hk/gia/general/199806/12/0612097
.htm

33 Hong Kong's "Captain America" Protester Jailed under National Security Law,
BBC, 11 November 2021, accessed at: https://www.bbc.com/news/world-asia
-china-59247659#

34 Hillary Leung, "I Go Almost Every Day": The Elderly Hong Kong Democracy
Advocates Following 2019 Protest Court Cases, *Hong Kong Free Press*, 13 February
2024, accessed at: https://hongkongfp.com/2024/02/13/i-go-almost-every-day-the
-elderly-hong-kong-democracy-advocates-following-2019-protest-court-cases/

35 Chung Kuang-cheng, Man Hoi Yan, and Emily Chan, Hong Kong Motorcyclist
Gets Nine Years for Flying Banned Slogan, Riding towards Police, *Radio Free
Asia*, 30 July 2021, accessed at: https://www.rfa.org/english/news/china/banned
-07302021125447.html

36 M.A., "Lessons in Dissent," A New Documentary Film, Tells the Story of the
Charismatic Young Founders of Scholarism, a Hong Kong Activist Group, *The*

Economist, 4 July 2014, accessed at: https://www.economist.com/analects/2014/07 /04/lessons-in-dissent

37 Ibid.
38 Tripti Lahiri and Mary Hui, A Timeline That Explains What's Happening in Hong Kong, *Quartz*, 16 August 2020, accessed at: https://qz.com/1890236/whats-happening-in-hong-kong-in-one-timeline
39 Hillary Leung, Then and Now: 79 Days of Protest in Hong Kong, *Time*, 27 August 2019, accessed at: https://time.com/5661211/hong-kong-protests-79-days/
40 Kelly Ho, Hong Kong 47: Activist Considered Quitting Primary Poll over "Broad Scope" of National Security Law, Court Hears, *Hong Kong Free Press*, 9 August 2023, accessed at: https://hongkongfp.com/2023/08/09/hong-kong-47-activist-considered-quitting-primary-poll-over-broad-scope-of-national-security-law-court -hears/. Tommy Walker, 4 Members of Defunct Pro-Democracy Party Arrested in Hong Kong, *VOA*, 5 July 2023, accessed at: https://www.voanews.com/a/members -of-defunct-pro-democracy-party-arrested-in-hong-kong/7168647.html
41 https://hongkongfp.com/2022/01/10/21-jailed-for-up-to-42-months-for-rioting -during-2019-hong-kong-protest/
42 Hillary Leung, Hong Kong 47: Democrats "Lacked Willpower" in the Past, Ex-Hospital Authority Union Chief Tells Court, *Hong Kong Free Press*, 23 August 2023, accessed at: https://hongkongfp.com/2023/08/23/hong-kong-47-democrats -lacked-willpower-in-the-past-ex-hospital-authority-union-chief-tells-court/
43 Ibid.
44 James Lee, "Unauthorised Article" Removed from Prison By Hong Kong Activist Was Complaint Form to Gov't Watchdog, Court Hears, *Hong Kong Free Press*, 31 October 2023, accessed at: https://hongkongfp.com/2023/10/31/unauthorised -article-removed-from-prison-by-hong-kong-activist-was-complaint-form-to-govt -watchdog-court-hears/
45 Lea Mok, Hong Kong's Pro-Democracy Businesses Tread Carefully as " Yellow Economy" Reels from Reported Arrests, *Hong Kong Free Press*, 8 July 2023, accessed at: https://hongkongfp.com/2023/07/08/hong-kongs-pro-democracy-businesses-tread-carefully-as-yellow-economy-reels-from-reported-arrests/
46 Ibid.
47 Timothy McLaughlin, Trump Is a "Necessary Evil" for Some, *The Atlantic*, 31 October 2020, accessed at: https://www.theatlantic.com/international/archive/2020 /10/democracy-activists-who-love-trump/616891/
48 Michelle Chan, Hong Kong Film Flirts with Political Controversy, *Nikkei*, 14 April 2018, accessed at: https://asia.nikkei.com/Life-Arts/Arts/Hong-Kong-film-flirts -with-political-controversy
49 Baggio Leung has since left Hong Kong and so has Nathan Law. Edward Leung after serving his sentence of five years, remained quiet because he was released under conditions of being stripped of political rights and free speech. Louise Watt, Ex-Hong Kong Lawmaker Baggio Leung Flees City for Washington, *Nikkei*, 11 December 2020, accessed at: https://asia.nikkei.com/Editor-s-Picks/Interview/Ex -Hong-Kong-lawmaker-Baggio-Leung-flees-city-for-Washington
50 Usually translated as "Liberate Hong Kong, Revolution of our time," the slogan was first used by Edward Leung Tin-Kei (梁天琦), the spokesperson of the pro-Hong Kong Independence party, Hong Kong Indigenous, in the 2016 Hong Kong Legislative Council by-election. Indeed, "liberate" may not be a very accurate translation of the Chinese term "光復," which literally means "restoring the light" or "restoring the glorious past." After protesters adopted this slogan in late July 2019, both the Chinese and the Hong Kong government condemned the protesters for inciting revolution and challenging state sovereignty, see https://hongkongfp .com/hong-kong-protest-movement-data-archive-glossary/

51 Mary Hui, The Leader of Hong Kong's Leaderless Protest Movement Is a Philosophy Student behind Bars, *Quartz*, 30 July 2019.accessed at https://qz.com/1678104/jailed-activist-edward-leung-is-hong-kong-protesters-spiritual-leader

52 Tong Syu Yuet and Gao Feng, Hong Kong Independence Activist Edward Leung Released from Jail, Told to Stay Silent, *RFA*, 19 January 2022, accessed at: https://www.rfa.org/english/news/china/jail-01192022123919.html

53 Hong Kong Film Group Cancels Public Screening of Protest Documentary, *RFA*, 15 March 2021, accessed at: https://www.rfa.org/english/news/china/film-03152021124457.html

54 Zen Soo, Hong Kong Prosecutors Allege Democracy Publisher Jimmy Lai Urged Protests, Sanctions against China, *AP*, 3 January 2024, accessed at: https://apnews.com/article/hong-kong-china-jimmy-lai-trial-ed8d33fb5f9828ad5ab6c72ed2a613f3

55 McLaughlin and Mahtani cite two precedents – Fang Lizhi, a scientist professor who was regarded as the "black hand" of the 1989 student movement by the CCP, and Chen Guangcheng, a blind activist lawyer. The first was at first refused help, but the decision was quickly reversed by then president Bush. Both were helped and smuggled out of the country. Tim McLaughlin and Shibani Mahtani, The Hong Kong Activist Who Called Washington's Bluff, *The Atlantic*, 4 November 2023, accessed at: https://www.theatlantic.com/international/archive/2023/11/hong-kong-activists-washington-dc/675693/

56 Pak Yiu, U.S. Refused to Help Joshua Wong Flee Hong Kong, Sources Say, *Nikkei*, 8 November 2023, accessed at: https://asia.nikkei.com/Spotlight/Hong-Kong-security-law/U.S.-refused-to-help-Joshua-Wong-flee-Hong-Kong-sources-say

57 Tim McLaughlin and Shibani Mahtani, The Hong Kong Activist Who Called Washington's Bluff, *The Atlantic*, 4 November 2023, accessed at: https://www.theatlantic.com/international/archive/2023/11/hong-kong-activists-washington-dc/675693/

58 *Media in Hong Kong*, chapter 2

59 Jimmy Lai's Views behind Editorial Decisions, *RTHK*, 5 February 2024, accessed at: https://news.rthk.hk/rthk/en/component/k2/1739265-20240205.htm

60 Pak Yiu, U.S. Refused to Help Joshua Wong Flee Hong Kong, Sources Say, *Nikkei*, 8 November 2023, accessed at https://asia.nikkei.com/Spotlight/Hong-Kong-security-law/U.S.-refused-to-help-Joshua-Wong-flee-Hong-Kong-sources-say

61 Kelly Ho, Hong Kong Activist Owen Chow Challenges Prison Ban on Book Containing Botticelli's Venus Painting, *Hong Kong Free Press*, 6 December 2023, accessed at: https://hongkongfp.com/2023/12/06/hong-kong-activist-owen-chow-challenges-prison-ban-on-book-containing-botticellis-venus-painting/

62 Hans Tse, Detained Hong Kong Activist Chow Hang-tung Allegedly in Solitary Confinement Again after Receiving "Too Many Letters," *Hong Kong Free Press*, 18 December 2023, accessed at: https://hongkongfp.com/2023/12/18/detained-hong-kong-activist-chow-hang-tung-allegedly-in-solitary-confinement-again-after-receiving-too-many-letters/

63 Tonyee Chow fans Facebook page https://www.facebook.com/ChowHangTungClub

64 Sebastian Veg, Hong Kong's Enduring Identity Crisis: 16 Years after the Territory Reverted to Chinese Sovereignty, Its Residents Feel Increasingly Uneasy with Beijing's Rule, *The Atlantic*, 16 October 2013, accessed at: https://www.theatlantic.com/china/archive/2013/10/hong-kongs-enduring-identity-crisis/280622/

65 Apple Daily English Aimed to Draw Foreign Support, RTHK, 20 February 2024, accessed at: https://gbcode.rthk.hk/TuniS/news.rthk.hk/rthk/en/component/k2/1741104-20240220.htm?spTabChangeable=0delete

66 Hong Konger: Jimmy Lai's Extraordinary Struggle for Freedom. *Supra* note 31.

67　Lai Wanted Bookseller Story to Boost Protest Turnout, *RTHK*, 19 January 2024 https://news.rthk.hk/rthk/en/component/k2/1736957-20240119.htm

68　Ibid.

69　*Apple Daily* English Aimed to Draw Foreign Support, *RTHK*, 20 February 2024, accessed at: https://gbcode.rthk.hk/TuniS/news.rthk.hk/rthk/en/component/k2/1741104-20240220.htm?spTabChangeable=0

70　Hans Tse, Hong Kong Prosecutors Present Apple Daily Front-Page Ad Saying "Freedom Has Become A Crime" in National Security Trial, *Hong Kong Free Press*, 19 February 2024, accessed at: https://hongkongfp.com/2024/02/19/hong-kong-prosecutors-present-apple-daily-front-page-ad-saying-freedom-has-become-a-crime-in-national-security-trial/

71　Brian Wong, Now-Defunct Stand News Portal Did Not Censor Articles By Bloggers Even If " Radical" Views on Hong Kong Expressed, Court Hears, *The SCMP*, 10 January 2023, accessed at: https://www.scmp.com/news/hong-kong/law-and-crime/article/3206330/now-defunct-stand-news-portal-did-not-censor-articles-its-bloggers-even-if-radical-views-hong-kong

72　According to sources who are familiar with the situation and preferred to remain anonymous.

73　徐沛然, "誰的主場？誰的新聞？論香港《主場新聞》關站事件' 苦勞網" 5 August 2014, accessed at: https://www.coolloud.org.tw/node/79584

74　Timeline: 58 Hong Kong Civil Society Groups Disband Following the Onset of the Security Law; HKFP Lists Which Civil Society Groups Disappeared in the wake of Hong Kong's Security Law, *Hong Kong Free Press*, 30 June 2022, accessed at: https://hongkongfp.com/2022/06/30/explainer-over-50-groups-gone-in-11-months-how-hong-kongs-pro-democracy-forces-crumbled/

75　Laura Mannering, Elaine Yu, Yan Zhao and Jasmine Leung, In Pictures: Hong Kong Is "Being Annexed and Destroyed By China," Says Independence Activist Andy Chan, *AFP*, 14 August 2018, updated 31 March 2020, accessed at: https://hongkongfp.com/2018/08/14/pictures-hong-kong-annexed-destroyed-china-says-independence-activist-andy-chan/

76　Hong Kong Refuses Entry to *FT* Journalist Victor Mallet, *BBC*, 9 November 2018, accessed at: https://www.bbc.com/news/world-asia-china-46148140

77　Hillary Leung, Human Rights Press Awards Axed after Stand News Wins; 8 FCC Press Freedom Committee Members Quit – Sources, *Hong Kong Free Press*, 25 April 2022, updated 17 August 2023, accessed at: https://hongkongfp.com/2022/04/25/human-rights-press-awards-axed-after-stand-news-wins-8-fcc-press-freedom-committee-members-quit-sources/

78　https://x.com/jamespomfret 2023.

79　司徒見林, "明報: FCC 主席承認取消「人權新聞獎」前與中國外交部視像會面並告知決定," *CommonsHK*, 1 June 2022, accessed at: https://commonshk.com/2022/06/01/明報: fcc-主席承認取消「人權新聞獎」前與中國外/. 聞風筆動: FCC大會有火花　主席取消新聞獎前告知外交部　/文: 李先知 . *Ming Pao Daily News*, 1 June 2022, accessed at: https://news.mingpao.com/pns/觀點/article/20220601/s00012/1654021502282/聞風筆動-fcc大會有火花-主席認取消新聞獎前告知外交部-文-李先知 . FCCHK internal bulletin to members; also stated on *Correspondents*, FCCHK quarterly magazine for members, accessed at: https://www.fcchk.org/press-freedom/

80　Chat with FCCHK member who preferred to remain anonymous for fear of reprisal.

81　Tom Grundy, Hong Kong Criticised for Barring Protest Photographer Michiko Kiseki from City, *Hong Kong Free Press*, 16 January 2023, accessed at: https://hongkongfp.com/2023/01/16/hong-kong-criticised-for-barring-protest-photographer-michiko-kiseki-from-city/; Kanis Leung, Japanese Journalist Barred from

Entering Hong Kong without Clear Reason, Newspaper Says, *AP*, 1 July 2023, accessed at: https://apnews.com/article/hong-kong-japanese-journalist-denied-entry-01efebdd8a503368bd0a3f79bcbd38d5

82 The author was an Executive Committee member, Hong Kong Journalists Association 2023–2024. She also served as an elected chairperson in the handover year of 1997–1998.

83 Holmes Chan, Scores of Hong Kong Journalists Injured during National Day Protests, as Some Outlets Recall Staff from Frontlines, *Hong Kong Free Press*, 2 October 2019, accessed at: https://hongkongfp.com/2019/10/02/scores-hong-kong-journalists-injured-national-day-protests-outlets-recall-staff-frontlines/

84 Tom Grundy, Journalist Shot in Face with Hong Kong Police Projectile Will Lose Sight Permanently in Right Eye, Lawyer Says, *Hong Kong Free Press*, 2 October 2019, accessed at: https://hongkongfp.com/2019/10/02/breaking-journalist-shot-face-hong-kong-police-projectile-will-lose-sight-permanently-right-eye-lawyer-says/

85 Interview with Ronson Chan, Good Morning Hong Kong Chat Show, *Radio Free Asia* Cantonese channel, 18 January 2022, accessed at: https://www.rfa.org/cantonese/talkshows/pltk/pltk-01182022081550.html

86 Tang Li-hang, reporter of *Taiwan Public TV*; Indonesian journalist with an eye injury – interview with HKJA.

87 Nominees for 2023 RSF Press Freedom Prize, 6 November 2023, accessed at: https://rsf.org/en/nominees-2023-rsf-press-freedom-prize

88 Timeline: 58 Hong Kong Civil Society Groups Disband Following the Onset of the Security Law, *Hong Kong Free Press*, 30 June 2022, accessed at: https://hongkongfp.com/2022/06/30/explainer-over-50-groups-gone-in-11-months-how-hong-kongs-pro-democracy-forces-crumbled/

89 HKJA membership – around 350 as shown on HKJA executive committee monthly meeting minutes, February 2024.

90 For further information on Ronson Chan, and the Hong Kong press freedom situation after the passage of the National Security Law see Danny Vincent, Hong Kong: Life under the Crackdown, *BBC*, 2 July 2022, accessed at: https://www.bbc.co.uk/programmes/m0018shr

91 https://hongkongfp.com/2024/02/22/hong-kong-pro-democracy-cafe-fined-hk3500-for-toilet-stains-after-owners-complained-of-weekly-inspections/

92 Tom Grundy, Hong Kong Press Group Says It Received Fresh HK$400,000 Tax Demand, with 6 Years of Accounts to Be Vetted, *Hong Kong Free Press*, 25 January 2024, accessed at: https://hongkongfp.com/2024/01/25/hong-kong-press-group-says-it-received-fresh-hk400000-tax-demand-with-6-years-of-accounts-to-be-vetted/

93 One of the authors is an executive committee member of HKJA and received the email.

94 1 徐沛然, ‘誰的主場？誰的新聞？論香港《主場新聞》關站事件’ 苦勞網 5 August 2014, accessed at: https://www.coolloud.org.tw/node/79584

95 Irene Chan, Hong Kong Pro-democracy Cafe Fined HK$3,500 for Toilet Stains After Owners Complained of Weekly Inspections, *Hong Kong Free Press*, 22 February 2024, accessed at: https://zh.wikipedia.org/zh-hk/獨立媒體_(香港)

96 Gov't Given Second Chance to Ban "Glory to Hong Kong" Protest Song, *AFP*, 23 August 2023, accessed at: https://hongkongfp.com/2023/08/23/govt-given-second-chance-to-ban-glory-to-hong-kong-protest-song/

97 Joe Chung, *I Don't Want to Be Chinese Again* (來生不做中國人) 允晨文化實業, 2012, accessed at: https://en.wikipedia.org/wiki/Joe_Chung

5 Concluding remarks

Concluding remarks

This manuscript attempts to discuss media, the internet, and the civil movement in Hong Kong as a case study, with a special focus on control mechanisms and protest strategies, informed by the theory of political economy of media and market.

Historical context

Hong Kong was once the promised land for the pursuit of autonomous rule under China's sovereignty. By the formula of 'One Country, Two Systems,' stipulated in the Sino-British Joint Declaration, an international agreement, Hong Kong would become China's Special Administrative Region in 1997, but would enjoy a high degree of autonomy. Hong Kong's people would run Hong Kong, largely free from Beijing's intervention, while its social and economic systems would remain unchanged for 50 years. With fundamental rights and freedoms ensured by law, and property rights protected, Hong Kong would remain a free capitalistic cosmopolitan city open to the world. Besides the promise that the pre-1997 status quo would be preserved for at least 50 years there were other undertakings: the Court of Final Appeal would have the power of final judgment, the Chief Executive would be returned by some form of election, and the legislature would be constituted by elections. In drafting the Basic Law of Hong Kong, the city's mini-constitution, Beijing went further and committed itself to the ultimate aim of electing the Chief Executive and the entire legislature by universal suffrage. Taken together, these commitments, if fulfilled, would distinguish Hong Kong from its colonial past as well as from other Chinese cities.

The new era, however, has turned out to be a contrary process of China taking full control. Departing from the original design, Hong Kong's journey into autonomy was short-lived and its search for democracy prematurely ended. In short, China as Hong Kong's sovereign, according to Beijing's version, holds unlimited power beyond challenge over the SAR. In the formative years, China was widely seen as practising a hands-off policy. The leadership

DOI: 10.4324/9781003150244-5

of the SAR Government was made up of Hong Kong's local people. No one would envisage that Beijing would step into Hong Kong affairs if it found a red line had been crossed.

In 2003, with massive mobilisation in a campaign against a proposed national security law from all walks of life, and in particular professionals, more civic groups were formed, civil society was activated, and the opposition camp was empowered. A popular pro-democracy movement had come of age.

On ideology and economy

The abandonment of China's hands-off policy began in the aftermath of the 2003 political crisis. Beijing sought to beef up its ideological influence in Hong Kong. Its objectives included promoting patriotism, boosting national identity, and enhancing nationalistic education. To further increase its influence, Beijing steered Hong Kong's economy towards greater dependence on China. Policies facilitated greater mobility of people, capital, and business across the border. Cross-border infrastructure projects were initiated to boost capacity for an increasing flow of visitors and goods.

As a result, China enjoyed substantial growth in its economic influence over Hong Kong. Mainland China emerged to top the ranks of both foreign visitors and investors in Hong Kong, while also remaining the largest trading partner for Hong Kong. In the financial market, Chinese enterprises became the leading group in Hong Kong's equity market in terms of both market capitalisation and turnover.

Democracy is postponed indefinitely

Powered by its absolute authority over the interpretation of the Basic Law, reinvigorated multi-layered networks of influence, policies of ideological indoctrination, and cross-border economic integration, Beijing struck back forcefully. The challenge of pro-democracy forces was contained. Beijing's blatant interference in Hong Kong, however, brought to life new tensions and strong resistance. The huge increase in mainland Chinese visitors, though beneficial to Hong Kong economically, also created social problems and conflicts.

In 2011, more than 35,000 mainland pregnant women took advantage of the easy access to Hong Kong after 2003 and came to Hong Kong to give birth, mainly in public hospitals. This was perceived as an economical shortcut to obtaining permanent residency for their offspring. These unwelcome developments created popular discontent and sparked growing protest actions against the parallel traders and mainlanders' "invasion." Worse still, it triggered an outcry for distinct separation from mainland China covering a wide range of issues, including preservation of culture, norms, and behaviour in this colonial enclave which boasted of its lawful and liberal way of living.

On the ideological front, while Hongkongers were reminded of their Chinese national identity by daily broadcasts of promotional videos and the playing of the national anthem before news programmes on TV, prominent pro-democracy leaders and activists were condemned by Beijing's media in Hong Kong as unpatriotic or undesirable elements who "oppose China, disrupt Hong Kong." National education in schools, likewise, aimed to enhance the sense of belonging to China by presenting a flattering view of China.

Politically, Hongkongers grew disillusioned as they realised universal suffrage was not a matter of time as stipulated in the Basic Law but required Beijing's approval. Beijing's subsequent decisions, first to postpone universal suffrage to 2017 and later to add a patriotism requirement for Chief Executive candidacy, confirmed Beijing's intention to deny democracy in Hong Kong altogether. To seize back what had been lost, some pro-democracy leaders concluded, Hong Kong's people must think outside the box and resort to collective action. Borrowing ideas from Mahatma Gandhi and Martin Luther King, one dominant view advocated the use of non-violent civil disobedience to press for change.

This line of thought led to plans for a pro-democracy movement, known as Occupy Central, a 10,000-strong peaceful sit-in protest to be held indefinitely on public roads in Central, Hong Kong's downtown, in 2014. Pro-democracy leaders hoped that mass support for the protest, along with transport chaos and international media attention, would compel Beijing to yield and allow universal suffrage. The Occupy Central idea, though law-breaking, was peaceful and orderly, widely appreciated and followed. However, thugs were hired to disrupt Occupy Central's activities through violence and to create fear among the public. As public support faded with time, the mass movement lost steam and died down after 79 days. The hope for universal suffrage was dashed.

Growth of localism

The forceful escalation of China's influence, intended to assert nationalism in Hong Kong, ironically fostered the growth of localism. Since the early 2010s, a handful of sporadic citizen campaigns had emerged, ranging from protests against the influx of mainlanders, to the demand for greater say over the China-Hong Kong relationship and the pursuit of universal suffrage as the safeguard against Beijing's interference. These led a small minority of dissenters to the idea of self-determination and even independence after the Joint Declaration expires in 2047. Less dramatic versions of localism sought to defend and preserve Hong Kong's integrity, including its core values, institutions, interests, identity, and heritage. They were different in their appeals and actions but all shared the common goal of resisting the threat from China to the values and causes they treasured most.

China, meanwhile, pursued its campaign against independent media. A news portal, *The House News,* for instance, which supported the Occupy Central campaign, suddenly closed down, just a few months before the movement kicked off. The portal owner was reportedly "frightened" as he found Hong Kong overwhelmed by a "white terror" atmosphere which brought unbearable pressure on him and his family. In established media, prominent radio phone-in hosts critical of the Beijing and Hong Kong authorities were fired. A senior editor of *Ming Pao* was sacked in 2016 after the newspaper published the Panama Papers, which showed how Hong Kong as an international financial hub served wealthy Chinese by moving money out of China. In 2014, the chief editor of the same paper was seriously injured by two hired attackers, after *Ming Pao*, in collaboration with the International Consortium of Investigative Journalists, disclosed the offshore holdings of China's business and political elite. On the book publishing front, the disappearance of five booksellers of Causeway Bay Books in late 2015, all of whom were later found detained in the Chinese mainland, spelt the end of Hong Kong as a centre outside China for publishing and selling books banned in China. The fact that one of them, Lee Bo, was arrested in Hong Kong by Chinese "special agents" and abducted to the Chinese mainland for detention, demonstrated China's willingness to be ruthless in silencing voices deemed "dangerous" by extra-legal means. As a result of all these frustrations, the "banned books" market in Hong Kong withered, investigative reporting on China-related sensitive topics diminished, and opposition media, if surviving, were run under severe economic and political pressures. Hong Kong's global ranking in press freedom plummeted from 18th place in 2002 to 73rd place in 2017, marking a significant deterioration over a span of 15 years. However, worse was to follow, reaching an all-time low ranking of 148th in 2022, two years after the enactment of the National Security Law.

Defeated, disillusioned, and divided, the pro-democracy movement after Occupy Central was at a low ebb. The cause of democracy was submerged. Five years later, the movement was revived and reinvigorated with unprecedented strength and solidarity when protests against the Extradition Law Amendment Bill (ELAB) broke out in 2019. The movement was at first a single-issue mass campaign against the Extradition Law Amendment Bill. Later, as the government repeatedly ignored million-people-strong demonstrations, rejected the popular request for investigation into police brutality against protestors as witnessed by mass media and human rights organisations, and refused to withdraw the bill, it evolved into a people's movement.

The pro-democracy camp's landslide victory in the district council elections of November 2019 further showed overwhelming support for the anti-ELAB movement by the populace. This tremendous success in local elections, which engendered strong public pressure against the repressive government, encouraged them to take a similar step again in the forthcoming Legislative Council elections in 2020. Beijing hit back with more ferocious repressive measures in the short term and the long term. While the police continued the brutal oppression of street protests, including the arrest of more than 10,000 protesters, lockdown measures due to COVID-19 banned public gatherings and stopped all kinds of protest activities.

Media blamed for the upheaval

One major device was the Beijing-enacted National Security Law (NSL), which was imposed on Hong Kong in July 2020. Since then, 47 pro-democracy candidates for the Legislative Council elections, who joined the election coalition mentioned above, were charged with conspiracy to subvert the state power. *Apple Daily*, a pro-democracy newspaper, was forced to close after seven senior executives were arrested and accused of conspiring to "collude with a foreign government", a crime under National Security Law, for publishing articles calling for sanctions against China and Hong Kong by foreign forces.

The Hong Kong Alliance in Support of Patriotic Democratic Movements of China, which had run annual vigils since 1989 to commemorate the bloody suppression of pro-democracy protests in Tiananmen, came under pressure in 2021. All seven members of its executive committee were arrested and remanded on different NSL charges. Its website was removed, social media accounts closed down and items on display in its June 4th museum seized, all by the authorities empowered by NSL. Eventually, the Alliance decided to dissolve in late September 2021.

With the demise of the Hong Kong Professional Teachers' Union, the largest teacher union, and the Hong Kong Confederation of Trade Unions, the only independent union coalition, the Alliance's collapse meant the authorities had removed the three biggest organisations in Hong Kong's civil society. Two years after the NSL came into force, it was estimated that about 60 organisations had dissolved. In order to stifle political criticisms not covered by NSL, the Hong Kong authorities revived the sedition offences inherited from the British colonial era, which were enacted in 1938 and unused since the 1970s. Netizens who expressed discontent with anti-epidemic measures for COVID-19, or posted banned political slogans such as "Liberate Hong Kong," were arrested on sedition charges.

A group of speech therapists who produced a series of children's picture books about sheep and wolves, metaphorically referring to Hongkongers and Beijing respectively, were charged with inciting hatred against the authorities. They were convicted and jailed for 19 months.

Two editors-in-chief of *Stand News*, a pro-democracy online platform, were arrested on charges of publishing seditious material for running articles highly critical of the government. The two editors were remanded in custody for about a year before being released on bail, but the news platform ceased operations after the police action. As of July 2023, more than 140 people had been arrested on National Security Law-related charges, with 94 of them facing formal charges.

Legal sanctions aside, the fear instigated by the national security regime helped spread mounting political pressure, encouraging self-censorship in all walks of life. Among its effects, the national security regime led to a lack of organisations willing to host commemorations for the Tiananmen Square massacre, a lack of news media publishing political cartoons, restrictions on the publication of books covering "sensitive topics," (some bookshops were forced to shut by administrative abuses – frequent check-ups and visits), libraries removing "sensitive" books, classroom teachers toeing the "party line", more movies being banned from public screening, and no labour groups daring to organise any public assembly on Labour Day. In short, political opposition was silenced, freedom of expression muted, and civil society dismantled.

Hallmark of 2019 movement: split between pan-democrats and radical youth

In chapter 3, we discussed the repressive measures used by top Chinese officials to change the system in Hong Kong, which traditionally combined capitalism with the protection of free speech and other human rights. In 2017, the Chinese Foreign Ministry declared that "one country two systems" had become void. But this was later contradicted by Xia Baolong, the top official in charge of Hong Kong and Macau affairs, who said that "one country two systems" still applied, but "one country" came first.

Domestically, there had been a prolonged internal split and controversy among the democrats – ranging from the pan-democrats to the radicals and militarists. The traditional democrats had been advocating the "compromise and criticise" strategy, accompanied by approval of the idea of reunification with China. The young activists were usually relatively radical when compared with the older generation of activists, and aspired to a higher level of autonomy – not just a high degree of autonomy but self-determination. They identified a Hong Kong ethnic group with its own indigenous rights, justifying various degrees of Hong Kong independence.

The sprouting of a local identity evolved from a polite assertion of cultural difference from mainland China to college student advocacy of the "if we burn, you burn with us" motto, with its overtones of self-sacrifice in order to cause mutual destruction (laam-chau) with the Hong Kong government as well as the Central regime.

Representatives of this included Gywneth Ho, journalist of *Stand News*, who openly announced in court that she was prepared to make sacrifices so China would react or over-react in a manner that would impose an even more austere and extreme policy on Hong Kong, and reveal to the world, the real nature of the Chinese Communist Party. This action and reaction eventually occurred. In support of the 2019 civil movement, and in protest at the following clampdown, a bill of sanctions was passed in the US targeting China and top Hong Kong government officials. In response, China swiftly imposed a mainland-style National Security Law without any local consultation, and downgraded Hong Kong to just another Chinese city, merging it into the Greater Bay Area with Guangzhou and Macau.

With this upcoming integration, and Hong Kong under the mainland's National Security Law since 2020, citizens are deprived of judicial protection, and have lost traditional Common Law benefits such as the presumption of innocence, the right to bail while awaiting trial, the right to opt for trial by jury in serious cases, and the defendant's right to choose his or her counsel.

As one commentator said, the hardware of the Hong Kong judiciary remains largely the same – the solemn setting of a British court, with judges and barristers wearing wigs and robes as in the colonial era, and traditional courtroom rituals. Innovations include flocks of security officers on guard inside and outside of district and regional level courts as well as the high and supreme courts, with lengthy security checks on bags and identity. Public justice is impaired by "queuing-up gangs" who are allowed to take up all the public seats in a courtroom, preventing relatives and supporters of the defendants and witnesses from getting tickets to go inside the main court and see their dear ones.

The two main democratic media, namely the print newspaper *Apple Daily* and the digital *Stand News*, have been forced to close, their offices have been raided, senior editors arrested, and bank accounts frozen. The chilling effect was apparent and intended. Fear spread among all media practitioners, journalists, and correspondents in Hong Kong. The demise of the two prominent pro-democracy media and the arrests of veteran journalists led directly to hundreds of journalists losing their jobs, and leaving the profession, or indeed leaving Hong Kong.

After the National Security Law was imposed, several changes in media and the journalism industry were noted. They were:[1]

- *Demolition of independent media*: Besides *Stand News*, *Apple Daily,* and *Hong Kong Citizen News*, several other Chinese-language media organisations closed, and some survivors have limited their operations, though some smaller outlets or individual journalists continue to publish on social media.
- *Journalists became political prisoners*: At least 40 journalists and media professionals have been charged with national security or sedition offences for their work, including *Apple Daily* senior editorial and managerial staff. owner Jimmy Lai, and senior staff at *Stand News*. And numerous journalists were injured while covering protests in 2019.

- *Hong Kong public broadcaster became state media*: As independent media were targeted by police crackdowns, the government worked to convert the once-respected public broadcaster *Radio Television Hong Kong (RTHK)* into a government mouthpiece. *RTHK* no longer has editorial independence. Staff have been threatened with financial penalties if they produce programmes that are later censored. *RTHK* deleted much of its pre-NSL content from the internet, depriving millions of residents of access to historic archives. *RTHK* has ceased to carry the BBC's news channel which it had been doing in the colonial era and for many years after the 1997 handover. Instead, in August 2021, the station partnered with Beijing's *China Media Group* to broadcast programming that would nurture patriotism.

- *Internet censorship and surveillance upgraded*: Hong Kong's people used to enjoy a relatively free and open internet before the introduction of the NSL, but internet censorship has become increasingly common. Pro-government lawmakers have urged the Hong Kong government to consider blocking access to the messaging platform Telegram under revised legislation related to doxing – the unauthorised release of personal information online. Even watching a documentary about pro-democracy protests on streaming platforms may constitute an NSL offence, and authorities are expanding their ability to monitor online activity. A law requiring residents to register their SIM cards under their real names has come into effect, replicating a system used on the mainland to track and arrest internet users.

- *Attempted erasure of Tiananmen from Hong Kong's collective memory*: In another shift towards mainland conditions, authorities have sought to erase Hongkonger's collective memory of the 1989 Tiananmen massacre, including banning the June 4th Museum in Hong Kong. The online "June 4th Museum," preserving the memory of Beijing's bloody crackdown on protesters in 1989, has become inaccessible via several of Hong Kong's major telecom providers. It came into existence after police confiscated all the exhibits at a separate, bricks-and-mortar museum in Hong Kong.[2] The long-standing annual vigil in Victoria Park has been banned since the NSL came into effect, and the area is now heavily policed in early June. Officials have also removed memorial statues at universities and restricted *RTHK* from reporting on the topic.

- *Fake news bill and enactment of Article 23, domestic NSL in 2024*: After the NSL imposition, the government of the Hong Kong Special Administrative Region (HKSAR) has been working on "fake news" legislation that could yield more criminal charges against journalists, closures of outlets, and self-censorship. This will follow the government's hasty implementation of an ordinance to conform to Article 23 of the Basic Law, which calls for local legislation prohibiting treason, secession, sedition, subversion, theft of state secrets, and links with foreign political organisations. The government is also reportedly working on a Cybersecurity Law to deal with national security threats online. The Legislative Council has been devoid of opposition members since a mass resignation in 2020 and the imposition of a repressive new electoral system in 2021. Any proposal originating from the government will likely be passed without close scrutiny.

In Chapter 3, we talk about the control measures exerted by the authorities, namely legal and extra-legal measures, including the powerful NSL, de-radicalisation and re-education tactics, detention of journalists in China, making witnesses out of activists by "torture," setting million-dollar bounties employing long-arm administration and extra-territorial rule by law, use of repeated administrative check-ups to force bookshops to disappear, and use of middlemen to harass, intimidate, and engage in visible stalking to scare journalists.

In Chapter 4, we examine how protesters and activists used social media and the internet to communicate, spread their message, and mobilise people at large to support their cause.

Enhanced by the universal ownership of mobile phones, the attempt at decentralising decision-making became an instant miracle, replacing the convention of relying on a prominent – usually pan-democrat – politician as a leader. The young protesters eventually groomed themselves from a sporadic dissident group to become an organised generation inspiring students, parents, professionals, and ordinary citizens from all walks of life, with their determination and fast-changing strategies and tactics.

For the record, there was a big rift between young protesters and the newspaper proprietor-turned-advocate for democracy. The main difference was that media proprietor Jimmy Lai had always been a friend of pan-democrat leaders, and a strong supporter of the Democratic Party, Civic Party, and other pro-democracy groups. He appeared in almost every vigil to commemorate those who sacrificed their lives in the Tiananmen crackdown in 1989, while professing support for the return of Hong Kong to China and the reunification of greater China.

The young activists, to varying degrees, tended to advocate Hong Kong having its own identity, separate from China, and being allowed to retain its own values, culture, and socio-political system. In the wake of the authoritarian clampdown, both the pan-democrats and the radicals came together to carry on the fight; members of both camps were arrested and detained starting from 2021, and put on trial in 2023 and 2024.

Prospects

As we said at the outset, the purpose of this research was to re-examine the political economy of media theory by using the case of Hong Kong. In 2019, we witnessed an unprecedented civil movement both historically and globally in terms of its geographical scope and its ability to rally the support of millions of mainly peaceful protesters for actions lasting from June to November that year. The impact continues. The media, though, have been comprehensively purged, with numerous important figures detained for two or three years before being brought into court on sedition charges in 2023 and 2024.

When we re-examine the power of media, we cannot underestimate the mobilisation factor in a civil movement and the lack of judicial protection after the return of Hong Kong 27 years ago to China. In the author's last study, "Media in Hong Kong," she mentioned the popular media, for instance, *Apple Daily*, as using market forces, namely the audience power, civil society, and professional journalism as strong countervailing forces to counter the enormous political and economic factors favouring the establishment.

More recently, the situation has become much more complicated than it appears. In the period under study, *Apple Daily* proprietor Jimmy Lai, generally regarded as pro-democracy and also a supporter of China's reunification, used his paper to advocate and lobby foreign support, and even call for international sanctions, particularly from the US, to curb the Chinese clampdown and to advance the cause of Hong Kong democracy.

However, Lai also experienced a change of mind: in the most fierce and rigorous confrontations, clashes and showdowns between the police, the peaceful and the valiant protesters, he chose to stand behind the young activists and asserted his authority by politely instructing his senior editors to play up the news reports by shedding light on the rather controversial violent acts or reactions on the part of the young protesters. Lai, as proprietor, was in a position to impose his wishes, but his instructions were, at times, met with reluctance from his professional journalistic team, if not occasionally complete rejection, or so they now say. For example, Lai wanted to implement a Democratic Party leader's recommendation of printing overseas politicians' ideas as prominent news, and he also wanted to invite overseas columnists to be regular contributors to *Apple Daily*. Worse still, he urged his senior staff to invite a writer who had already exiled himself to Taiwan to contribute as a columnist. The op-ed page editor thought this writer was likely to advocate "Hong Kong independence" so he thought the idea was risky after the promulgation of the National Security Law in 2020. So he followed his independent judgement and quietly disobeyed the order.[3]

Similarly, when Lai proposed setting up a new English edition of the *Apple Daily* in order to better spread Hong Kong news, and better recruit support from American politicians and ordinary citizens alike for Hong Kong's quest for democracy, he was met with objections. A famous columnist, Chip Tsao, denounced the idea in print, saying it was useless in the first place, and secondly, it might invite criticism for inviting foreign forces to intervene. Later it emerged in a court hearing that the idea of setting up an English edition of *Apple Daily* was proposed by another columnist, Fung Hei-Kin. There was a big argument behind the scenes before the objection was revealed to the public at large.

Chip Tsao also suggested *Apple Daily* should shut down voluntarily in order to save senior staff from getting into trouble, saying that *Apple Daily* had performed its historic duty and discharged its responsibility. But the paper continued to print on Lai's orders even after he was charged and remanded in custody. It was only after the bank account of *Apple Daily* was frozen and more senior staff were arrested that the associate publisher announced the paper would be shut down. On the last day, *Apple Daily* printed a million copies and they were sold out completely, demonstrating readers' support for the popular newspaper until its final day.

The economic factor had indeed cast a strong adverse effect on the daily. It lacked advertising revenue even though it was the leading mass-circulation daily in Hong Kong. There was nothing mysterious or economic about this: former HKSAR Chief Executive Leung Chun-ying named and blamed those companies who dared to put advertisements in the opposition paper. However, the daily could survive the financial crisis by attracting support from readers' subscriptions once it went digital. Indeed, in 2018, when Lai made a comeback after leaving the paper to be run by his management between 2009 and 2017, he made an important switch of emphasis by turning *Apple Daily* from a mainly hard copy publication to having 70% of its staff working on the digital version.

According to court testimony from Lai's CEO and publisher, Cheung Kim-hung, Lai started to engage in the newspaper's editorial decision-making in 2014, when hundreds of thousands of residents took to the streets to demand democratisation in the Umbrella Movement, or "Occupy Central", in which Lai himself participated. "It was a watershed moment," Cheung said. "Since 2014's Occupy Central, *Apple Daily* had seemingly become an anti-government, anti-Central [authorities] newspaper. Since then, *Apple Daily* had walked down this path, and the management had followed Lai's directions in running the newspaper." The court has so far heard allegations that the former media mogul was the "mastermind" who orchestrated the alleged conspiracies, using the now-closed *Apple Daily* as a platform and providing instructions and financial support to his aides to lobby for international sanctions.[4]

Although the newspaper incurred strenuous political opposition, Lai was not deterred and persisted until he had been in prison for more than 1,000 days, both his personal and company bank accounts had been frozen, and his senior editors and management had been arrested and detained. Under these circumstances, his paper could not possibly continue.

The saga of *Stand News*

On the digital media front, the leading online media *Stand News* was informed by various sources that it would be the next to be shut down after the *Apple*

Daily. However, the chief editor strove to continue the online news as long as possible, while preparing for the worst. He resigned from acting as the chief editor of *Stand News* only after his wife, the former deputy publisher of *Apple Daily*, was arrested and detained by the police. He promoted his long-term right-hand man to acting chief editor while he redeployed himself as finance controller. They continued to print investigative news reports, such as the Panama Papers story. But the fate of the digital *Stand News* was similar to its democratic counterpart *Apple Daily*. It was forced to shut down after its two chief editors were arrested, followed by the freezing of the company's bank account.

Market mechanism fails to act as countervailing force

Economic forces were not enough to counter political pressure on the media under authoritarian rule.

After the 2019 civil movement, Hong Kong, once a relatively liberal city-state, has been under repressive political force to turn it into a mainland-style Chinese city with no opposition voices. The market mechanism lost steam as the audience could not exercise their rights of speech or choice, and could not use financial forces to support the democratic media in whichever way they wished. A once mature civil society, with all kinds of civic institutions and diversified media across the political spectrum, has been steamrollered into a narrow space in which only pro-establishment voices are heard, only patriotic organisations are tolerated, and there are no more political parties, non-governmental organisations (NGOs), or civil institutions to provide critical information or opinions.

The transition of Hong Kong into a normal Chinese city will be complete soon, including having Putonghua as the only official language, rather than the centuries-old Cantonese language. Due to decades of mass immigration from the mainland, non-local students now routinely fill half of university classes, a local undergraduate complained. International statistical comparisons also show that the level of freedom in Hong Kong has recently dropped to a level similar to that of Tibet.[5] An important political development is that the European Council has decided to treat Taiwan as a separate entity from China, saying that the two have no political connection.[6] On the other hand, China has given up the hope of using Hong Kong's "one country, two systems" model as an attraction to lure Taiwan into talks on reunification.

Prospects for the media

At least 40 journalists and media professionals have been charged with NSL or sedition offences for their work, including *Apple Daily* owner Jimmy Lai and his senior staff, and chief editors at *Stand News*. There are over 1,000 political prisoners in total, including those convicted for protest-related activities.

Faced with such repression, many Hongkongers have fled into exile. Some journalists and activists have created diaspora media outlets like *Flow HK*, *Commons*, and *The Chaser* to cover Hong Kong news and serve the burgeoning exile community. Increasingly there are famous Hong Kong writers and journalists setting up their own channels overseas and speaking up on Hong Kong issues. The trend will be similar to but not exactly like what happened in the 1960s, 70s, and into the late 80s when China started to embark on economic reforms and allowed a certain degree of media freedom. During China's Iron Curtain period, Hong Kong played an important role in publishing forbidden news to the world such as the number of deaths in the great famine in the 1950s and the political struggle during the Cultural Revolution from the mid-1960s to the mid-1970s.

In this connection, the overseas digital news channels will become more important if they continue to maintain professional standards. Sooner or later, the news covered abroad will become what happened in China before, that is, the Hong Kong news will be "exported and then imported" back to the local Hong Kong audience. Domestically, while the major democratic media fell, Hong Kong's professional journalists started to form their own we-media on a small scale and have been covering news in specific areas such as court news, social, and entertainment news. Political news seems to be a big void, discouraged by the fluid and uncertain red line of national security law.

Next target of control: The shrinking political space on the internet

An economist's prediction, "Hong Kong is over"[7] was echoed by the US Consul General in Hong Kong and Macau, who suggested that the authorities should consider releasing Jimmy Lai and other political prisoners if they wanted to rebuild a free city in Hong Kong and improve the city's economic prospects. But Consul General Gregory May predicted that Hong Kong would impose even harsher controls on the internet, including setting up a China-style Great Firewall and curbing free use of the internet. At the moment, he noted that American business people were wary and used "burner" cell-phones and separate computers in order to protect their privacy and prevent their personal data from leaking.[8]

In short, the trend is indicative that China no longer treasures Hong Kong as an economic and finance information hub, which in past decades helped China to attract investment, technology, and information about the outside world. Apparently, China's only concern is with the integration of Hong Kong into China, making it succumb and dissolve into the "one country" norm, which is socialism with Chinese characteristics, rule by China's law, party media, and patriotic legislators. The once pro-China economist mentioned above is very disappointed and also believes "Hong Kong is over." Some academics would further conclude that the unprecedented political experiment of "one country, two systems" for Hong Kong has failed. The rest is history. From the perspective of local journalists, this is the worst time but also the best time in the history of journalism. Recently, there is a phrase repeatedly posted on Facebook which may express the spirit of the 2019 civil movement: "It's not seeing hope that makes you persevere, but rather persevering that allows you to see hope." A free but undemocratic city-state, Hong Kong's path has never been smooth and direct. Rather, it has been detouring and eventful. As long as the residents can maintain their stamina, the story of Hong Kong is far from ending.

Notes

1 Angeli Datt, Hong Kong Is Unrecognizable after 2 Years under the National Security Law, *The Diplomat*, 20 June 2022, accessed at: https://thediplomat.com /2022/06/hong-kong-is-unrecognizable-after-2-years-under-the-national-security -law/

2 Rhoda Kwan, 1989 Tiananmen Massacre Online Museum Blocked in Hong Kong, Three Weeks after Police Raid Physical Site, *Hong Kong Free Press*, 29 September 2021, accessed at: https://hongkongfp.com/2021/09/29/1989-tiananmen-massacre -online-museum-blocked-in-hong-kong-three-weeks-after-police-raid-physical -site/

3 Columnist Sang Pu was turned down by the op-ed page editor, Li Ping, who feared that the columnist's enthusiasm for Hong Kong independence might get *Apple Daily* into trouble, according to Chan Pui-man, former associate publisher and an accomplice witness for the prosecution. Jimmy Lai Instructed *Apple Daily* to Find Pro-independence Writers While in Custody, Court Hears, *The Standard*, 27 February 2024 , accessed at:https:/ /www.thestandard.com.hk/breaking-news/sect ion/4/213807/Jimmy-Lai-instructed-Apple-Daily-to-find-pro-independence-writ ers-while-in-custody,-court -hears;

4 Hans Tse, Jimmy Lai Trial: Media Mogul Instructed Apple Daily to Mobilise Protests, Urge Sanctions, Ex-Publisher Says, *Hong Kong Free Press*, 18 January 2024, accessed at: https://hongkongfp.com/2024/01/18/jimmy-lai-trial-media -mogul-instructed-apple-daily-to-mobilise-protests-urge-sanctions-ex-publisher -says/

5 Alex Willemyns, Report: Freedom Continued to Erode in 2023, *RFA*, 29 February 2024, accessed at: https://www.rfa.org/english/news/china/freedom-house-report -02292024150218.html

6 European Council – saying Taiwan is a different political entity from China, 歐洲議會 (European Parliament) 強調台灣中國互不隸屬　中方斥無知要「多讀書」, *RFA*, 1 March 2024, accessed at: https://www.rfa.org/cantonese/news/htm/tw -european-03012024014217.html

7 Stephen Roach, It Pains Me to Say Hong Kong Is Over, *Financial Times*, 12 February 2024, accessed at: https://www.ft.com/content/27a2c28e-d28b-444c -97fd-4616ed32c675

8 Alan Wong and Sarah Zheng, Top US Envoy in Hong Kong Warns of Creeping Internet Curbs, *Bloomberg*, 2 March 2024, accessed at: https://www.yahoo.com/ news/us-envoy-warns-hong-kong-030040132.html

Afterword

By Carol P. Lai

The idea of writing a follow-up to my last book popped up amid all the sweat and tears in mid-2019. When I doubted whether anyone would want to read about Hong Kong, Professor James Curran urged me to write, as there was much interest in the UK.

Routledge first agreed to publish the book on the 25th anniversary of the HKSAR in 2022. When the National Security Law was imposed in July 2020, we sensed a threat to the free press but we did not know how far it would go. With hindsight, it was lucky we missed the deadline.

We postponed the deadline to 2023, hoping to include the *Stand News* trial and the *Apple Daily* trial. But the trials dragged on into 2024. We could not afford to omit these two important media cases, but final verdicts are still awaited.

I wish to thank all the friends who shared their insights. As no one wished to be mentioned for fear of reprisals I cannot thank anyone here, including my angel editor friend. My co-author made the difficult decision to leave his beloved Hong Kong two years ago, apparently due to the changes horrifying all of us here.

The past three years seemed frozen in time due to COVID-19 and related restrictions. I lost my teaching job, as well as my radio programme. The public broadcaster's excuse for shutting down all locally produced chat shows was telling – "they fear we fear." I would wake up in the middle of the night, feeling the absolute solitude friends and acquaintances must be experiencing in their custodial cells.

I wrote and discarded two drafts. Then I started to attend the court proceeding of the *Stand News* trial, followed by the *Apple Daily* case at the beginning of 2024. There I saw ordinary citizens braving the cold to queue up for a ticket to the main court, and passing the ticket to the defendant's loved one who could not get one because the "queue-up gang" had taken all the tickets. There are many more such stories still unwritten.

I would like to thank my co-author Andrew, the editors at Routledge, and Hannah for their patience in this ordeal. Any faults in this work, if any, are mine. Lastly, I take the liberty to dedicate this book to K, HT, GH, CM, MC, LF, Lai's family, and all our unfortunate colleagues.

DOI: 10.4324/9781003150244-6

Index

For Product Safety Concerns and Information please contact our EU
representative GPSR@taylorandfrancis.com
Taylor & Francis Verlag GmbH, Kaufingerstraße 24, 80331 München, Germany

www.ingramcontent.com/pod-product-compliance
Lightning Source LLC
Chambersburg PA
CBHW060408290526
45791CB00002B/663

9 780367 713010